SELECTING YOUR MATE

By V. A. Sutton

Order this book online at .selectingyourmate.com
Also available through major online retailers

© Copyright 2011 V.A. Sutton

Selecting Your Mate: Second Edition
All rights reserved. No part of this publication may be reproduced, stored in a retrieval system, or transmitted, in any form or by any means, electronic, mechanical, photocopying, recording, or otherwise, without the written prior permission of the author.

Printed in the United States of America

ISBN: 978-0-9996-194-0-7 (hc)
ISBN: 978-0-9996-194-1-4 (sc)
ISBN: 978-0-9996-194-2-1 (e)

Library of Congress Control Number: 2018905681

VAS Publishing rev. 05/09/2018

VAS Publishing
North America and International
Phone number (585) 489-1409

WE ATTRACT HEARTS

BY THE QUALITIES WE DISPLAY

WE RETAIN THEM

BY THE QUALITIES WE POSSESS.

Jean Baptiste Antoine Suard

Selecting Your Mate is an excellent guide for a young person who is seeking a "Christian Mate".

R. Dorsey

Healthcare Professional

Marriages are often entered into lightly, merely responses to individuals' most urgent infatuations, ideals, needs, wants, and lusts. Whether couples remain married—or not—the consequences of such unions are disastrous, not only for them, but also for their children, extended families, friends, and communities. More than an interesting read, Selecting Your Mate provides practical, scriptural guidelines for identifying appropriate marriage partners in order to establish and maintain lifelong personal and marital bliss.

R.D. Watson,
Assistant Professor
Monroe Community College

DEDICATION

TO MY CHILDREN WITH LOVE

A note from the author

First and foremost, I am thankful to the Lord for all things. Creating a desire within me to express the many issues of concern surrounding the selection of a mate has been a challenging opportunity. Obstacles that are placed in our path are simply episodes of unique encounters that produce the special journey in life upon which we travel.

One of the most valuable experiences that life offers is the ability to learn. Wisdom is designed to renew the mind. With an appropriate insight, you restore new possibilities for personal growth. This will help you determine how to contend with difficulties that appear in courtship. When knowledge is revealed, the true value of a significant lesson can then be received. A much deserved blessing can only become your reality once you decide to eliminate the cycle of repeated failure. Relationship challenges will continue to exist until you recognize the symptoms that lead to these problems. Only you can take the proper steps to conquer the battle these issues present in your life.

Sincere thanks goes to everyone involved in the effort to help me publish this work. Your encouragement has been an inspiration for me to be steadfast in publishing my thoughts. I have finally completed a meaningful task which has taken several years to compile. Now, I realize that if I can help somebody along the way because of my life experiences, then my writing has not been in vain.

Author's Note: All names in this book are fictitious and do not reflect any actual situations or events.

Author Reflections...

As a Wedding Planner and Special Event Designer for over thirty years, I have been granted the greatest gift ever...a working knowledge in areas that are best learned through actual experience. Exposure to diverse cultural and social environments has prepared me with a creative ability to improvise and manage activities on the spot. The interaction between couples that leads to their special wedding day helped to provide an interesting awareness about their future.

In reflection, different beliefs that shape attitudes for marriage were innocently revealed and I stumbled upon unique learning experiences from every opportunity. The basic groundwork that was needed to uncover an understanding about the importance of selection came into focus. This knowledge was more than just preparation needed to work through planning or handling of an event; but was also related to unforeseen circumstances that lead to a foundation for marriage.

Within the frame of these very personal occasions, the personal likes and dislikes of each client come into focus. As part of the planning process you naturally develop an extraordinary bonding which connects you to each couple in a special manner. These interactions represented real-life examples of what is necessary to develop the process for having a successful relationship without the fear of failure. The experience brings into view many different influences upon marriage.

Growing up as the minority gender within a family, gave insight to the unique perspective which helped me to rethink important information that is often overlooked and misunderstood about the importance of identifying love. Throughout those memorable interactions with siblings, there were many occasions upon which distinctive behavior patterns were observed. These incidents reminded me of the importance of our social environments and how we develop our attitudes toward lifetime decisions.

In view of selection choices, decisions that are based solely upon physical desires do not have the strength needed to endure relationship challenges. Once the physical appearance changes so do the psychological needs. Another influence upon ideas regarding marriage was most often passed on from elder relatives or person's held in high esteem to an individual. Communication with peers also makes a great impression upon how you understand the subject of "Love."

When a person looks upon the same set of events, at the same moment in time and does not come to a similar conclusion it reflects your ability to independently position oneself to think before action is taken. Being a concerned parent that has experienced the joy of marriage and the pain of divorce, I have boldly taken this opportunity to speak to the hearts of young adults. The process of selection requires that you must rely upon more than what appears to be your reality.

Awareness of your beloved's intentions is more than just the impression of qualities that are believed to exist, but moreover the ability to determine if an individual's character is truthful. You must learn to observe and not forget this unmistakable information, for it is crucial in your decision. The example of his or her behavior should never escape your thoughts in the selection process of your mate.

Introduction

The selection of a mate is a decision that will hopefully be made at some point. This is a decision that will not only affect an individual's life but also generations to come within everyone's family. A process for selection is of great concern because there are so few relationships that have success "until death do we part". The circumstances referred to by this statement involve the natural longevity of a relationship, not one that is induced through actions of violence.

Selection has become an interesting topic of discussion. People have so many different ideas surrounding the manner in which we make choices. First time around decisions for a mate have become increasingly obsolete as American society prospers on the dysfunction of marriages. Considering who will be your partner in holy matrimony is a sensitive issue that can no longer be ignored.

Divorce ranks high as the prominent resolution for our personal failure in relationships. Alternative lifestyles are on the rise as state after state paves the way for same sex unions. With all of the threats that impact the stability of family in today's society, we must not forget that the "marriage union" is the most complete relationship a man and a woman could possibly have. The future of our culture rests upon its existence. We must, therefore, restore order and prevent the thoughtless behavior that prevails in marriage today.

As we evaluate the truth about the selection of a mate and a matrimonial commitment, it will help to understand why this is a crisis. Marriage is more than just moments of pleasure; it's the continuation of life. The decision process that leads to selection of a mate should not be taken lightly but with careful thought and consideration. To abandon the freedom of being single for a new lifetime commitment of uncertainty is not unrealistic. When you believe the time has come to settle down, the idea of marital obligations will challenge your thoughts. A transition in thinking begins when sharing your life with someone overshadows what used to be the comfort of being alone.

Now as the search begins, where is the beginning? Many questions will come to mind when examining the realities of wedded bliss. What is the potential for this marriage and will it work? Can this relationship be the lifetime commitment I truly desire? Will this marriage be a matter of convenience, or is it based upon expectations that are false? How will I know if I truly love this person or that he or she is in love with me? Am I just a romantic fanatic hung up on the idea of being in love without a desire to truly make a commitment to anyone?

You will determine the answer to these questions when you understand some basic principles about marriage. An approach to selection is impossible without having this information. Every decision that is made has a moral or legal impact that will embrace your being. Sometimes this occurs in ways that you never imagined. Whether the result is an intelligent or foolish alternative, each situation is a distinct learning experience. Hopefully you can accept the outcome. However you come to a form of reasoning about the choices you make, the conclusion should arise from sound and reliable knowledge.

As you make changes in your selection process, please acknowledge there are consequences for not holding on to those truths that free us from wrong. The desire for wedded bliss will no longer remain a difficult task as you begin a transformation in thinking. A different point of view about whether someone has the potential to be your mate is important, and having the advantage of great wisdom will sharpen your insight on basic selection realities.

In the beginning of a courtship, conclusions are made about the manner in which someone may behave or conduct themselves. These thoughts are viewed as a tendency for actions that set the stage for later. A person's conduct will imprint upon our mind a routine which is expected. For example, holding the door open; going out to dinner; or other gestures of affection such as unexpected gifts. The other side of this behavior, which is not readily seen, could be a display of selfishness, lies or unwarranted jealousy. Whatever mode of interaction a person practices, these attitudes are generally anticipated to continue to exist within the marriage space.

Once you understand this timeless battle, "when we were dating you used to ..." the reality becomes clear. The only difference between a person in marriage and the person you dated is your perception. These two images are the same. The difference is what you have overlooked. Now that your time and attention have been obtained, it would not be expected that either of you would change in your attitude for love. There are some BASIC PRACTICES you need to know to ensure wise decisions. This will help you make better choices in the early stages of courtship. Too often a person becomes legally bound to someone only to find out later that there should have been more time spent in getting to know him/her.

A selection decision is best made when a couple is equally confident in their knowledge of each other and has similar expectations to build a good, strong base for commitment. Marriage is not an option to cure whatever is troubling a relationship. The sooner you recognize how to make decisions based on the realities that stand before you, the easier the search for a mate will become. I hope you enjoy reading <u>Selecting Your Mate</u>. Whatever you conclude from the contents of this book, there is one thought that remains constant…

Your entire life can be altered by a simple choice.

Table of Contents

A note from the author... ix

Author Reflections….. xi

Introduction.. xiii

I. Making A Decision…..1

II. In The Beginning……………………………………………...37

III. Getting To Know…..61

IV. Once You Understand…..91

V. The Mating Game…..117

Chapter 1

MAKING A DECISION...

No longer are you those little children of yesterday, seeking my help because you need guidance.

This is one road that I cannot travel upon with you as this journey will take you into a new phase of your life. You will hear people share expressions of wisdom from their personal dating encounters. Although these courtship ideas are believed to be a correct course of action; sometimes the thoughts of others provide limited expertise. This is proven every time singles persist in searching for a mate.

Without trustworthy facts, the unmarried continue to explore mating options. Old wives tales and husband tales of past times do not always provide quality wisdom. Dating etiquette continually changes to accommodate the latest courtship craze. An unfortunate result is the manner in which courtship standards are viewed relating to romantic behavior. Single couples have adopted sensation-seeking behaviors with the intent of identifying someone to become a potential mate.

Acceptance of these sometimes outrageous attraction techniques have started a trend of reasoning that has spiraled out of control. With our tolerance of unpleasant behavior, singles have gotten away from an attitude that reflects what the definition of love truly means. The conduct of the unmarried relating to matters of the heart is often communicated in a way that confirms they are misinformed about how to identify sincere affection. This behavior is not limited to any particular age group.

As a matter of fact, an amusement park was closed on a holiday weekend due to reported threats of potential violence. The closing transferred problems to a different location…a community festival at the beach. Families enjoyed the weather while the air was filled with the distinct aroma of meat being barbecued and the sounds of laughter which reminded folks that warmer days had finally arrived. However, these moments of enjoyment were quickly interrupted with reported fighting amongst different groups of people.

How disturbing to learn that among these offenders were thirty year old women. Surprisingly, the age ranges varied from teenagers to adults. There was a talk show discussion that reported how the parents of younger children were disappointed with increased violent trends that were invading their public opportunities to have a simple family outing. The disorder at these events immediately made the environment of the festival change. As police intervened, fearful families left… end of holiday.

These events bring one concern to mind, "Where is the love?" After having numerous conversations concerning courtship and marriage relationships, it ceases to amaze me the lack of knowledge most individuals have surrounding the manner in which they will find someone to love. As most people continue to believe false ideas about affection; they tend to get further away from the reality of being able to identify what love truly means. Once you understand the principles which are characteristic of the standards for love, a natural selection can be made that is worthy of your intentions.

This particular story was shared with me about the way an adult person envisioned love in his life.

A vivid childhood memory that I recall was about our neighbor Wesley. He would abuse his wife on a regular basis as if it was a ritual. I finally asked his wife Barbara one day;, "Why do you allow your husband to beat you up?" Surprisingly she responded with this statement; "When a man beats a woman baby, don't you know that is his way of letting you know that he loves you."

On another occasion there was a man named Nate, who was constantly getting beat upon physically. The attacker was his spouse Patricia. These unpleasant confrontations made marriage life quite difficult. Sounds strange, but believe it or not it happens. Whether physical, psychological or sexual, abuse is not exclusive to any particular gender or victim. In this case, Nate stated he had never retaliated against his wife because his dad taught him a man never hits a woman…

A young couple named Kevin and Anna stated that throughout their courtship there was only one occasion in which both remember having a disagreement. There was one instance of simple dispute.

After several years of settling into the marriage and before having children, there was no condition that challenged this rapport. Within their personal interactions no arguing existed because of mutual admiration, but moreover a loving respect which the two attribute to the success of the relationship.

Their special love included continuous communication with the Lord as part of their daily routine.

The nature of this couple's relationship did not allow threatening obstacles from outsiders to disrupt marital happiness, first built upon friendship. They both made a conscious effort to maintain this practice throughout the marriage. Misunderstandings were not a part of their lifestyle as they both respected each other's opinion without allowing "anger" to invade their

Making A Decision...

relationship space. Much too often this happens without the knowledge that this emotion can be the destructive agent to any relationship.

When a person wants to sincerely communicate affection to you, there is reinforcement with actions as well as verbal confirmation that informs you of their intentions. Do not allow yourself to become a victim of agendas that leave you vulnerable because you believe someone loves you, when in reality they are deleting you from their equation. There was a case in which a young woman fell head over heels for her first love. This young man became a special friend with the intention of gaining her confidence.

After becoming sexually active for the sake of "love", the young man walked away without looking back as he walked into the arms of another. This young man was not ready to honor a one on one commitment in a relationship. The young woman "assumed" the feelings would eventually be shared, but that was not the case. Now that her heart was broken, where do you go from here? This daily scenario happens to men and women. The solution is not to put "you" in this position.

Mutual friends were confused about the outcome of this courtship as everybody thought they both loved each other. Socially, it became uncomfortable for both to interact within the same circles. As this painful reminder set in, the unfortunate reality about character came into focus. You really can protect your heart from emotional disaster. Make sure you understand the difference between a real friendship and a casual association. Think through your set of circumstances by relying upon the perfection of wisdom which simply states:

> *A friend loveth at all times...*
>
> **Proverbs 17:17 (KJV)**

For this reason, the advantage of dating is to keep the "getting to know" phase in place for as long as it takes to discover whether this is true love or a charade of affection. In either case, the true agenda will naturally surface. There's something about the practice of doing wrong; it cannot tolerate that which is right. What purpose is there in entertaining time with someone whose intention is to attack your spirit with their unhappiness?

> ***Put on the whole armour of God that ye may be able***
> ***to stand against the wiles of the devil.***
> ***Ephesians 6:11 (KJV)***

For any individual whether male or female which falls prey to the challenges of romance; refer to these things and know the Lord will provide spiritual protection against any adversary. He will help you overcome temptations that take you away from actions which glorify God. Keep in mind, that through the strength of Christ all things are possible. The price to discourage your happiness has no value except for the one with this purpose…to be the author of confusion.

Leave no room for someone's immature behavior to become your emotional suicide that takes control of the peaceful frame of mind you have, and replace it with conditions that eliminate the prospect for joy to take place. After asking the following question of different people, I recognized that the true motivation for writing these thoughts is justified by a need. The following question was asked to many couples, "If you could do it all over again would you marry the same person?"

Surprisingly, this is one subject that took no time for consideration. There was no doubt in the minds of those asked regarding the answer to this question. The responses were all an immediate reaction; consistent with the circumstances that drive the conditions for their particular relationship.

This was amazing to me because in each case there was no room for debate. For each couple only one spouse was questioned because asking both

Making A Decision...

simultaneously would be another book. The reply being positive or negative revolved around the same reasoning ...the selection of their mate.

Comments such as this: "If I only knew then what I know now" or "If I had to do it all over again I would have married a different person" or "I would not have gotten married if..." These remarks were commonly made by people who believe their happiness is based upon another person's ability to create happiness in their life. Couples that have been married over fifty years were content with their spouses and would refer to another fifty with the same person. They have truly captured love.

The state of both persons being happy together was based upon individual choices that were created from self-imposed conditions. Couples that have fun together enjoy each other's company, but moreover are happy with themselves as individuals first. You control a destiny for happiness with the satisfaction of your existence.

> ***Happy is the man that findeth wisdom and getteth understanding...***
>
> ***Proverbs 3:13 (KJV)***

Proper efforts were not taken to ask the right questions or learn necessary information. In the courtship stages of a relationship, when a person's integrity comes into view in a manner that leaves a question in your mind, more than likely you need to stop...drop ...and roll. "Stop" all forms of conversation with the person. "Drop" the interaction because it is not going in the direction in which you want to travel. "Roll" on to a better relationship opportunity. You will find this to be the best call of your judgment when you can finally recognize another's character.

Kevin and Anna used wisdom when they put the Lord in the headship position within their marriage. This means that the two became one in their reliance upon the Lord for discernment of personal matters. As a result of confidence in Him, coupled with regular meditation and truthful communication, Kevin and Anna developed knowledge in the unchanging insight of biblical wisdom. This gave stability to the relationship as they learned from divine testimony to remove "self" early on.

There are times when a person has an insatiable need to actually experience events in order to better understand the reality of the consequences, rather than learn from the mistakes of others.

Just like the child whose parent tells he or she not to touch a flame because of getting burned does not stop the curiosity of putting their hand near the flame. You feel the warmth and when you get too close you begin to feel the burn. In either case, there exists a strong desire to do something other than what you have been instructed.

The foundation for love is learned through the evidence of wisdom in the scriptures. Biblical writings bring knowledge about a way of life that is "fool" proof when properly understood in accordance with the Lord's will. The failures we see in selection have countless beginnings and some of these originate from opinions with no logical meaning. Oftentimes wisdom is ignored because a person wants to rely upon his or her own understanding. Unfortunately, that is when the real trouble begins.

A basic difference in personalities affects compatibility within a relationship. Having the capability to get along with a person creates the natural balance necessary for doing and thinking as a couple. Without conformity there can be no harmony. When entertaining a special affection for another person, especially when there are thoughts of a marital commitment, it is important that these two people agree on standards which relate to behavior that will influence their life as a couple.

Love has quite an attracting force as it takes an effect upon you like the flow of a gentle breeze. Be mindful of the knock you off your feet lust

Making A Decision...

that catches you off guard with the surge of unexpected emotion. These feelings have the great potential to control you through thoughtless reactions. The difference between love and lust is the effect it has upon our human nature. There are people that truly believe in love at first sight; especially when they feel that special twinge in the heart. The next thing you know is that the courtship turns into a marriage union.

The better reality about this matter called "love" is that a proper selection was made as it should be. When you consider the actual circumstances surrounding how one finds love does it seem likely that a person can totally fall head over heels in love with someone he or she does not know? Love at first sight would mean physical attraction constitutes love. Shift your mindset to understand that behavior is the actual magnetism that appeals to your mind before you fall in love.

Take these thoughts for the sake of comparison to help you better separate the difference in your mind. This point of view greatly impacts how you differentiate the measures you use to determine the difference between affection and attraction. In either case, both can be a temporary condition when there is no basis of truth to rely upon. There are special characteristics to look for when you are in pursuit of that true love connection. Consider these points of interest as you adjust your awareness.

First of all, be confident in your initial assessment. Otherwise you could just fall in love with a mannequin that is clothed and doused with sweet smelling perfume simply because of the way it looks. The behavior of a person is important as it relates to nonverbal communication about the person. There is a distinct difference between physical attraction and the behavioral tendencies.

With initial feelings of affection, there are some things that you should look for that will stand up through the tests of time because they are the true source of a person's being.

The interest you have in someone unknown to you should only be acted upon with knowledge. You need to know who you are dealing with. There are so many different patterns of behavior that have been influenced by mass media forums until you think someone is attractive for the wrong reasons as you search for love. Let's continue to seek wisdom that identifies specific patterns relating to the manner in which someone should behave. This will help you discern with careful forethought whether a person qualifies for entrance into an area which is your most valued part — your heart.

As the center of your emotional life, this element has a strong influence upon one's character. The controlling force of our powerful nature is important to understand. You will find that within these protected chambers lay the person you really need to know. It is important to also recognize the inner motivation that drives a person's emotional and spiritual character. Remember the exposure to different events in our lives leave an impression upon the mind that has a lifelong memory.

These imprints can take form in a way that drives behavior. You never know what compels a person's reaction in a given manner at any time; therefore, the statement that anybody can be or do whatever his or her heart desires takes on a different meaning. It is interesting to think about how much of our life revolves around the condition of the heart. A decision to love is a choice that is made because of feelings that arises from a strong heartfelt emotion.

When you are drawn to someone, you believe the state of that person's heart is a reflection of his or her behavioral tendencies due to the things he

Making A Decision...

or she says. Typically, a kind-hearted individual is viewed as sympathetic with a calming, yet gentle nature. He or she seems nice because they care.

Most people are drawn to what they perceive to be the personality of this person. Yet, on the other hand when you see an angry person the first thoughts are the disposition is mean spirited or the individual is difficult to deal with because of a troubled mindset.

Wisdom shows us this…

> **"Harden not your heart."**
> *Hebrews 3:8 (KJV)*

A hardened heart is a mentality that will cause a person to make many mistakes. The most common mistake is an unbelieving attitude towards God. This is a crucial piece of evidence that should stand out as a precaution to you. The heart manages intellectual thoughts which determine how we deal with different areas in life. Differences as simple as forgiveness or not forgiving others are thoughts within the character that frames the attitude by which a person is directed.

The heart, being referred to as the mind and soul of a man, is the basis of affection towards another. It takes a special quality within both individuals to mutually work together to tolerate short comings of their beloved in an unconditional manner. Just because you seem to have a tolerance for some of the distinctive characteristics of another's reality does not mean you are compatible choices for a harmonious marriage union. Please consider this information seriously before taking steps to marry.

You must first decide if a person has the special qualities, not that you desire but which make an appropriate selection for what you seek as a potential "love" connection. Upon doing so, you determine if this person is right for you. Through personal insight of your own, which is coupled with a correct understanding of the attributes to seek, you can make an appropriate selection. For this process to occur, you must know the traits to look for in order to distinguish if they exist.

Over the course of time, within your courtship you will know if this person is the right fit for you.

Seeking these simple truths should be the standard for your decision process. Although the manner by which an individual chooses to handle his or her daily life affairs is a personal choice, it says a lot about whom they are personally. Regardless of circumstances, it is a mistake to continue walking on a path knowing you can never make the situation applicable to the life you want…

Aaron and Laura dated for six months prior to getting engaged. The plan was to marry within the year. Every possible moment was spent together getting to know each other while settling into a pre-marital mindset. They spent so much time together until there was little opportunity to think independently about whether marriage was the right course of action for them. In this relationship, there was a whirlwind of events that transpired in a short time span; with no break to contemplate whether they were suitable for one another.

Laura helped Aaron downsize his apartment as they prepared to make the transition into their marital living accommodations. Aaron made sure he discarded any remnants of other women from his bachelor days. His fiancée, Laura, took it upon herself to help while indiscreetly looking for more things to learn about her man. There was nothing that seemed out of the ordinary or would create any thoughts of suspicion about another person.

Making A Decision...

In the meantime, Laura actively helped Aaron get rid of unnecessary junk. You know those things that he had accumulated over that lengthy period of time which was spent as a bachelor. There were large trash bags full of empty beer and liquor bottles that she assumed were left over from parties and other gatherings with his friends. Laura did not drink, so she asked Aaron about the excessive bottles. He told her the bottles were never taken in for deposit and this task was on his to - do list.

Aaron never mentioned he was still indulging in a drink every now and then and of course, Laura never asked. Aaron continued to drink with excessive binges that led to him becoming extremely intoxicated and uncontrollable after their marriage. Laura ignored this crucial piece of information about her fiancée. Later on there were troubling incidents between her and Aaron. During marriage, the relationship changed because of too much alcohol consumption which altered Aaron's behavior.

Once he became drunk and out of control, Laura had no tolerance for his irrational actions. When she disapproved of his drinking, it was seen as persistent nagging. Her lack of acceptance radically challenged the direction of the marital relationship. Laura blamed their problems on the way Aaron acted after excessively drinking. There was a difference in Aaron's attitude. He in turn challenged Laura's concern for his drinking with different issues that the two did not mutually agree upon.

Aaron returned to his association with friends who wanted to party. Laura claimed that if she had known Aaron had these drinking problems, there would have been no wedding. Aaron feels that Laura was not critical like this before they married. Yet prior to marriage the reality stood before both of them. Neither person acknowledged these differences in lifestyle habits could become a major problem in their relationship until too late. This is the result of premature selection decisions.

The information Laura needed to know about her fiancée, now husband stood before her in due time. But for most people this information is ignored because of the overwhelming desire to have companionship. You control selection by taking the time to carefully assess your decision. This requires conscientious steps are taken. There is less opportunity for a risky union when there is more understanding about the person you will spend your life with.

What do you look for that makes the behavior of an appropriate suitor stand out? Must a person experience hurt before any learning can take place? Consider how much thoughtless selection in friendships also interferes with courtship when influence by association makes you settle for bad choices. Friendship represents your connection to others and reflects the general opinion of how you, as a person is known more deeply than ever realized. Most people relate to the manner by which you live through your personal behavior and the associations you maintain.

Your conduct is in a roundabout way viewed as similar to the mindset of the people in which you interact. This also relates to your willingness to be trustworthy. A wise person selects friendships that will co-sign in making intelligent choices. To be associated with people who are thoughtless and reckless in their behavior is quite destructive to your character. Nobody knows this any better than our heavenly creator who instructs us on all accounts.

> ***He that walketh with wise men shall be wise: but a companion of fools shall be destroyed.***
> ***Proverbs 13:20 (KJV)***

The analogy of a foolish person is quite simple. It is someone who refuses to listen to divine wisdom. This person is not only unreasonable in attitude, but can be identified by his or her expression of self-importance. There is no fear of being involved in activities which lead to wrongdoings. So dealing with this type of mindset will eventually end with you suffering from the association. You do not want to personally stumble from the negative influence of a lost soul...

> *The fear of the Lord is the beginning of wisdom: a good understanding have all they that do his commandments...*
>
> *Psalm 111:10 (KJV)*

Lack of fear is one of the most prevalent problems that young people face today. Finding the one special person who has respect or reverence for God with a "sincere fear" is preferred. For this reason, you will be able to serve the Lord with a dual sense of strength and purpose. Through your fear a sense of devotion is magnified. Decisions that are based upon these principles provide stability for both of you in your intentions to serve the Lord. This clearly defines the reason for you not to waste time with any kind of relationship.

> *Be ye not unequally yoked together with unbelievers for what fellowship hath righteousness with unrighteousness? And what communion hath light with darkness?*
>
> *II Corinthians 6:14 (KJV)*

This is a crucial point of wisdom for Christians who are truly seeking an appropriate mate. There will be a cause and effect result for any instructions that relate to your walk as a Christian. When you place yourself in a marriage with one that does not trust in God, there is a lack of belief and understanding for moral and spiritual truths. This companionship is a suicide to the soul when it weakens your faith with conditions that challenge your focus on submission to the Lord's will.

When your steadfastness is tested, it is not an easy journey. These edifying instructions forewarn you by forbidding a marriage relationship with a mate who is "not equal" as a believer. He or she is not of the same mind, which is a powerful testament of truth. This should be the basis by which you should make a distinction about commitment to a marriage union. With your journey in serving the Lord, how can this individual be a bond of strength in the relationship when he or she is weak?

This is a crucial piece to the understanding of whether there can be harmony as a couple. When you have a commitment to the same religious view points, your service to the Lord as a couple will be magnified in strength. Take the time to seriously consider why this distinction was made to help you determine if this can be an appropriate mate. The reference to darkness refers to the sinfulness towards anything that unites Christians with those who refuse to believe Gospel teachings of Christ.

You understand that there is no light in darkness because you cannot see. Spiritual blindness also represents that inability to see where a person is going because the truth is not in them. Their path is unfamiliar to you because of a lack of direction that exists for respecting divine truths. When you become added to the body of Christ you take on a heavenly light by nature of baptism. Cleansing causes the state of your heart to be visible and not hidden from others when your purpose is to serve the Lord. As your light shines, it pleases God, for He defines the conditions for righteousness.

Christians that have married outside of the faith will not admit their decision was good, unless their marriage partner actively embraces Gospel principles. You must be conscientious about risking your future with someone who does not trust God. Unbelievers are not equal with you for many reasons.

Making A Decision...

The most important being they are faithless children with no moral commitment to spiritual truth.

The only one that can change the heart of any man or any woman is God.

Behavior is the most overlooked key which unlocks the door to knowledge about a person. The special qualities you seek in someone to spend your life with are not manufactured on an assembly line like a selection of parts. Let's see, "I" want this in a mate, and of course "I" want that in a mate. Everyone comes in "as is condition" which they do not automatically change to comply with your personal expectations. A change in awareness for selection will help you realize that preparation for a "marriage partner" status takes a lifetime of learning. This stage in life varies for each individual.

It takes more than a spontaneous emotional reaction for a lifelong bonding to be created. A natural tendency is acquired through observation and upbringing. This mutual connection will be the solidifying force between you and your beloved as those personal characteristics that attracted you in the beginning will withstand the tests of time. These feelings come as a result of behavior that defines the reason you chose to love one another…

A couple dated a year prior to marriage and waited 12 years before having children. This gave them plenty of time to grow in their relationship. After 30 years of marriage, one partner decided upon a divorce. What could possibly have brought them to this point in their life? Had they grown apart or did they fall out of love? Although their problems could be traced back for many years with some pre-existing differences, this decision does not have a biblical justification for ending marriage.

The importance of selection before marriage is not stressed enough. Marriage was created by God and giving up on this relationship is not an option except under a certain condition — infidelity. The problem that marriage unions face today is way-out measures of the world for a relationship formed by the Lord. Consequently, the desire to continue these unions became a great struggle as couples lean less upon the Lord for direction, and the creator of marriage is no longer a part of the solution.

Within the courtship phase of the relationship, differences in biblical opinion were not identified as a source of problems that could negatively impact the frame of mind one has regarding ideas on a marriage relationship. The primary advantage of courtship is to understand who you are dealing with in terms of character, social interaction etc. Moreover, be sure the relationship is a worthwhile investment of your emotional time, before the decision turns out to be an error of choice.

There is one concern that can quickly destroy a love connection before it has a chance to blossom.

This is a behavioral reaction that cannot be ignored as unimportant, and it is envy. Reflecting upon feelings of jealousy will bring many experiences to mind for everyone. Being human, it is a feeling of insecurity that tends to surface when you care for someone whether you admit to it or not.

What is unfortunate about envy is how it brings out a side that promotes behavior which can lead to uncontrollable reactions from an individual. This is especially true of those eager to love someone.

The source of envy within a courtship relates to an imbalance of feelings in which one person cares more for another. Bible wisdom gives thoughtful learning that describes how someone's feeling of jealousy influences emotional behavior. Everyone has experienced a perceived rivalry directed at someone over the attention of a loved one whether competition is valid or not between individuals.

Within the space of any relationship, there is the potential for someone to become overly protective.

A love connection will have moments in which either person's feelings can be tested for whatever reason. When out of control, jealousy becomes the negative part of human nature because it is known for its impulsive reaction that can cause problems when the relationship allows envy to infiltrate emotional boundaries. The line of reasoning that surrounds this factor is a perception that an individual wants someone or something belonging to somebody else.

> *"For jealousy is the rage of a man..."*
> *Proverbs 6:34 (KJV)*

Jealousy, an intense emotion is impacted by the dedication to a commitment. Once you upset the perception of promise with a lack of respect, you will find consequences get out of control with a reaction that is greatly influenced by this emotional state. Rage has the potential for extreme violence because of its intensity. Therefore a combination of rage and vengeance become unstable emotions that are overpowering. Pushing someone to the point of rage is not a desirable condition.

Your values come under attack when your capability to be levelheaded is challenged with emotional decisions. An example of this can be seen anytime you turn on reality television shows. There is a portrayal of drama in which the participant's personal dilemmas become the public playground for unhappy singles. Couples have the opportunity to air the drama in their lives for the world to witness and in many cases intensify the rage. The popularity of these media streams is so great it is replacing the run of soap operas that were always popular during daytime television.

Take a moment and adjust your sound volume to minimum settings to observe facial expressions and the body language. With waves of emotion, arms fly about and nostrils flare to reflect a very negative social interaction. It speaks a lot about these individuals and their display of unhappiness. These gestures resemble a form of confusion that does not demonstrate appealing communication between these people. Watching couples publicly perform their reaction to private matters in a way that resembles a form of primal mating needs, must cease as it transfers wrong ideas.

Both genders resort to aggressively establishing their point of view. Visualizing such force in their attitude on a regular basis incurs a shift in the perception of what constitutes normal interaction. A lack of respect is becoming the acceptable behavior among the young when dating. Arguing or fighting over someone in public is now a common reaction which allows you to visualize how participants have been impacted. These out of control circumstances alter the outlook of American dating traditions.

In communities of the past, we were raised to handle personal and private affairs in a respectable manner behind closed doors. Now we have transformed interaction into a state of chaotic confusion that is not limited to the young. More incidents are reported with out of order communication exchanges that bring about the unpredictable. Unfortunately, the learning experiences from this approach transferred into the next generation with a vibrancy that seems never ending. With this exposure, we find intensified communication that further evolves in the wrong direction, and the cycle continues…

The following is a disturbing incident that reinforces how much these events impact even our teen youth. A young man launched a stabbing

Making A Decision...

attack against a former girlfriend on a vacant aisle in a large grocery store chain in a prominent neighborhood. Luckily, there were two male high school students in the store who became involved to help the victim. They subdued the assailant which saved this young teenage girl's life. The teenage men were hailed as heroes by local authorities...

At an apartment complex in a suburban community there were two females in junior high school fighting over a young man's attention. One student stabbed the other with repeated efforts. There were comments by outsiders to this community which foolishly stated, "Was there a parental presence in the home?" How does this disorder continue to exist when there are both parents living together in the same household "raising their children" with concerned direction?

Two male university students with promising futures got into a brawl over another female student. The fight ends fatally for one of the young men. These devastating circumstances were not only horrific for the families involved but moreover the community which is deprived of the potential success record of achievement from these young people. The great example these young men displayed for those who will come after them has now become part of the succession of violence that plagues all communities...

A five year old kindergarten student went to school and stabbed a classmate with a pencil several times because of anger...

Rage is a disturbing factor that does not end with these incidents only, but is the idea from which this violence originates. At some point the realization must be, no *more excuses accepted*. There has been such a breakdown in conveying values because we no longer talk; we text. This alone gives incomplete opportunities to fully express an opinion or engage in quality conversations which ensure that information is being clearly understood by the recipient for whom the message was intended.

A conversation with an educator revealed that many students have difficulty with assignments because they cannot verbalize thoughts on paper in an organized form. The ability to communicate for some, has become as limited as the abbreviated messages on the phone. As a result there seems to be less concern to converse thoughts verbally within a more relaxed setting or in a relationship. In order to assess a potential interest in someone there must be an ability to express ideas and engage in some form of dialogue where you convey your feelings through an exchange of ideas.

Furthermore, to understand what is appropriate behavior in your search for love it is important that you understand what cannot be done. The wisdom book shows us the conditions that are to guide our moral behavior within the old testaments 18th chapter of the book of Leviticus. Examples of behaviors between persons closely related are all detailed as an abomination to God. These are actions which are the result of impure, sinful natures that cause you separation from God. This is not a desirable position to be within …without God.

When the Lord spoke to Moses he told him to tell the children of Israel, "I am the Lord your God." He informed Moses to comply with the following divine cause which the Lord clearly defined. There are certain relationships that are not to exist because they constitute incest, which is sexual behavior between closely related relatives. These clearly defined actions are not behavioral practices that are acceptable. Leviticus shows us these immoral actions because they are shameful to the Lord and to avoid participation to guide the management of better lifestyle practices.

"None of you shall approach to any that is near to kin to him, to uncover their nakedness.

The nakedness of thy father, or the nakedness of thy mother, shalt thou not uncover; she is thy mother; thou shalt not uncover her nakedness.

The nakedness of thy father's wife shalt thou not uncover: it is thy father's nakedness.

The nakedness of thy sister, the daughter of thy father, or daughter of thy mother, whether she be born at home, or born abroad, even their nakedness thou shalt not uncover.

The nakedness of thy son's daughter, or of thy daughter's daughter, even their nakedness thou shalt not uncover; for theirs is thine own nakedness.

The nakedness of thy father's wife's daughter, begotten of thy father, she is thy sister; thou shalt not uncover her nakedness.

Thou shalt not uncover the nakedness of thy father's sister; she is thy father's near kinswoman.

Thou shalt not uncover the nakedness of thy father's brother; thou shalt not approach to his wife; she is thine aunt.

Thou shalt not uncover the nakedness of thy daughter in law; she is thy son's wife; thou shalt not uncover her nakedness.

Thou shalt not uncover the nakedness of thy brother's wife; it is thy brother's nakedness.

Thou shalt not uncover the nakedness of a woman and her daughter; neither shalt thou take her son's daughter, or her daughter's daughter, to uncover her nakedness; for they are her near kinswomen: it is wickedness.

Neither shalt thou take a wife to her sister, to vex her, to uncover her nakedness, beside the other in her life time.

Also thou shalt not approach unto a woman to uncover her nakedness, as long as she is put apart for her uncleanness.

Moreover thou shalt not lie carnally with thy neighbor's wife, to defile thyself with her.

Thou shalt not lie with mankind, as with womankind; it is abomination.

Neither shalt thou lie with any beast to defile thyself therewith: neither shall any woman stand before a beast to lie down thereto: it is confusion.

Defile not ye yourselves in any of these things: for in all these the nations are defiled which I cast out before you

Leviticus 18: 6-24 (KJV)

A couple should be able to co-exist in harmony with an emotional union that naturally cancels out whatever attempts are made against happiness. In other words, you should not allow yourself to be put in a position where you constantly struggle to compel another person to care for you. The

Making A Decision...

objective is to be involved in an effortless interaction that flows instinctively without challenges. In order to recognize these practices; you must also apply them in your life.

Singles have been hoodwinked into forgetting these patterns of behavior by allowing the ways of the world to influence what they should be looking for to identify special qualities that distinguish ones potential for marriage. With this uncertainty come poor selection choices. How do you recognize when you have found that promising spiritual connection that is important in the success of your marriage relationship? Oftentimes a person does not know what distinctive qualities to seek.

Within the character there are particular habits that make someone stand out to you as attractive.

To make a sound choice your selection decision must be based upon scriptural inspiration that will reveal what you need to make a determination. Your confidence must be built upon the evidence of wisdom that is not subject to change at any time. This is a primary example of why divine guidance is necessary for an effective influence upon the selection decisions that we make.

The Lord's design for marriage also incorporates the answers to mate selection. Here are some interesting factors for you to consider within the information you seek. When someone becomes a potential love interest, that individual should not be kept from family and friends as though a confidential secret. Withholding this person's identity is not only disrespectful to your family but moreover to yourself. The worst part of this action suggests there is darkness, and I have something to hide.

A relationship's secrecy is the absolute guarantee there will be problems further down the road.

Concealing the existence of a relationship is only advantageous for the person who will benefit the most from this information not being disclosed to family. There tends to be a greater indication that a person is either married, or covering up information they do not want uncovered by your family and friends. The objective in courtship is for a person's intentions to be made public in order to avoid the kind of vagueness that is not a normal pattern to follow within an appropriate courtship.

In the development of an appropriate relationship, it is the responsibility of a male individual to state "his" purpose in view of the possibility for marital plans. Men who decide to take a wife have studied and observed many things about this particular woman in advance to his personal interest being made known to this person. The idea of selecting a lifelong companion develops as an instinctive decision which is not prompted by anyone else's natural impulse.

A desire for marriage will not be decided by someone who is on the outside of the relationship. The assessment of a mate should be made with understanding of how to progress through the process of selection with complete confidence that you made the right choice. The following information highlights wisdom for learning basics on selection. Inspirational statements such as these are reliable evidence of how the decision becomes an accountability action for each gender.

With the understanding that both individuals have their unique part in the decision making process gives a different perspective to the manner in which you arrive at a conclusion. You will find that the way to successful selection involves more than personal insight, but the all-knowing wisdom of God. These particular instructions relate exclusively to the male responsibility and will validate confidence in the success of your decision. Effective selection requires an awareness of the truth. For the woman of choice, that agrees to become your wife there are specific instructions as well.

> *"Whoso findeth a wife findeth a good thing, and obtaineth favor of the Lord"*
>
> *Proverbs 18:22 (KJV)*

This desire has an order. Finding a wife indicates a search has been done to meet or come upon this individual. In some cases a man may learn of this woman by stumbling upon her acquaintance. A wife, being the woman to whom a man can marry indicates that a female is a qualification that is necessary for this choice to be made. Also notice that "a wife" is a singular designation which does not mean more than one at the same time.

Selection is ultimately the choice of a man. The male is primary in managing the search effort to acquire his own spouse. Man's responsibility in finding his wife gives him accountability with the Lord for his decision. The scriptures do not suggest that a woman who findeth a husband findeth a good thing. An unsolicited introduction by someone else has no bearing upon the outcome of these circumstances. Each man must find his own "qualifying" wife and will do so by whatever means.

For a man to find "a good thing" is based upon personal search actions. The value in finding "a good thing" suggests that he will receive something special, "favor" which is pleasing acceptance by God. The nature of a man is such that he knows and "recognizes" what he needs as opposed to what he wants. Obtaining favor is an action indicating the Lord is delighted when "a good thing" is finally found. God did not mean for man to be alone, so he created for him a help meet.

Having undeserved kindness upon the decision reinforces the divine endorsement of selection which is another significant aspect for the man. When making a selection, one must confidently understand how to recognize the spiritual character of his wife. Proverbs 31 discusses the profile of a good woman. Her importance in the marriage partnership is equally important to the achievement of a healthy marital relationship.

> *Who can find a virtuous woman? For her price is far above rubies. The heart of her husband doth safely trust in her, so that he shall have no need of spoil. She will do him good and not evil all the days of her life. She seeketh wool and flax, and worketh willingly with her hands. She is like the merchants' ships; she bringeth her food from afar. She riseth also while it is yet night, and giveth meat to her household and a portion to her maidens. She considereth a field, and buyeth it: with the fruit of her hands she planteth a vineyard. She girdeth her loins with strength, and strengtheneth her arms. She perceiveth that her merchandise is good: her candle goeth not out by night. She layeth her hands to the spindle, and her hands hold the distaff. She stretcheth out her hand to the poor; yea, she reacheth forth her hands to the needy. She is not afraid of the snow for her household: for all her household are clothed with scarlet. She maketh herself coverings of tapestry: her clothing is silk and purple. Her husband is known in the gates, when he sitteth among the elders of the land. She maketh fine linen, and selleth it; and delivereth girdles unto the merchant. Strength and honour are her clothing; and she shall rejoice in time to come. She openeth her mouth with wisdom; and in her tongue is the law of kindness. She looketh well to the ways of her household, and eateth not the bread of idleness. Her children arise up, and call her*

> *blessed; her husband also, and he praiseth her. Many daughters have done virtuously, but thou excellest them all. Favor is deceitful, and beauty is vain: but a woman that feareth the Lord, she shall be praised.*
>
> *Proverbs 31: 10-30 (KJV)*

In your search for that special virtuous woman, you must understand there are defining qualities to look for which exemplify the nature of this woman. A virtuous woman is one that has the unique strength to behave in an honorable manner. She is honest and maintains a moral integrity which means she will not engage in sexual promiscuity but remain committed to her partner in marriage. The value this woman brings to her husband's life is priceless. She will not make him ashamed by bringing shame or disgrace upon him with her behavior. The nature of her conduct sets a standard for excellence.

> *A virtuous woman is a crown to her husband: but she that maketh ashamed is as rottenness in his bones.*
>
> *Proverbs 12:4 (KJV)*

The crown is a symbol that denotes quality or the highest achievement. It also distinguishes the behavior worthy of respect and honor. This excellence makes a man proud as head of household. Finding that righteous woman is a great accomplishment which denotes there is value in attaining the reward of a wife. She cares for his needs and works with him on all concerns and situations. A woman that disgraces her husband with disastrous circumstances does not have confidence in God.

If the wrong selection is made in a wife, this woman becomes an element that will break down the strength and value of the union. For a man to be ashamed with rottenness, relates to the lack of moral integrity that is displayed when a woman disgraces her husband through her behavior in public. There is an unspoken status that is associated with a man finding a wife. Through the steadfast action of searching and finding a wife denotes maturity, responsibility and wisdom which are then perceived as honorable actions.

When there is persistence in seeking out somebody, it suggests that someone is worthwhile. I refer to this as the "hunt" in the game. The motivation for this hunter is to search for something special in someone that he wants. Sometimes it takes many years, but eventually he will stumble upon what he desires. An imitation or a prototype temporarily suffices, but is not the real thing and the search continues until she is found. Understand that a desire for someone should be two-sided.

Besides being the hunter, the hunted wants to be caught; otherwise there would be no reason for the pursuit. A decision is something that you own and for that reason the benefit of any conclusion comes with the realization that you have crossed over into a mature way of thinking to make an appropriate selection. This means you have left childish ideas behind as you mentally prepare to consider a mate. The process becomes a natural order as your ideas develop about selection.

Now that you are ready to acknowledge the impact this decision has upon your life you can take the experience to help you determine the final part of selection. Remember the process. In the beginning phases of the courtship, you came to fully understand that there are specific relationship responsibilities placed upon you as a man and also as a woman. These distinctive differences were purposely set forth by our creator with a special intent…companionship, submission to one another and to reproduce offspring upon the earth for the continuation of your combined family heritage.

Making A Decision...

Selection of a mate involves your making an informed choice. Getting to know another person without consideration of the visual beauty many look for in the physical demonstrates maturity. The importance of spiritual attributes should remain at the top of the list for qualities that you seek regardless of the circumstances. These common sense concerns in your thinking will remind you that "What you see is not always what you get" when all is said and done.

It takes time to get to know someone in those private and personal matters that display who the real man or woman is as an individual. Once your thoughts are aligned regarding the basic process to selection — getting to know — and you make a decision, you are ready to seriously evaluate the defining factor that completes your assessment of selection. This part is the subject of greatest concern — "LOVE".

In order to understand what love is, you need to understand the actions which display its meaning from both perspectives. Those that are not acceptable and do not define love as well as those that are an example. There are many thoughts on this topic and what you need to secure in your mind is the truth. How do you recognize whether it exists for you? To what extent must it be displayed before you make your mind up and believe you found this thing called love? Is there a way to truly identify these feelings beyond a reasonable doubt? Once love is found, is it possible that you can grow out of love for someone?

The best approach to understand our feelings is to distinguish how some thoughts are temporal and subject to change depending upon the circumstances. For example, someone can love the taste of milk until one day out of the ordinary it makes you sick. Maybe it was sour, or you could have developed an allergic reaction to the product. Does your point of view totally change about milk because of this experience or is there a temporary adjustment to your feelings because circumstances were out of your control?

When you consider emotional feelings, they typically relate to a response towards another person. "I love you because ..." is an expression based upon an action. As long as the action continues, then so do the circumstances surrounding love. When love changes in its pattern of action, the response to the action is different. "I don't like it when you ..." is a reaction to an unexpected change in external conditions. An outlook is altered from its original position as the actions change.

These are temporary influences that are a response to a specific set of circumstances. This is not a example of how true love works. Authentic love is not a conditional emotion that is qualified by the state of affairs that exist at the time. Love is a consistent pattern of behavior that will never fail. For this reason you must know the person you find, or that finds you will have the natural essence for those things which balances your emotional scale.

In I Corinthians 13:4-13, the apostle Paul writes about the characteristics of love. The words flow with such a beautiful poetic effect that it grips the mind with intense wisdom that empowers you with a higher height of understanding love. As I reflected upon these words, it occurred to me that the definition of love is more than just feeling affection. There is a particular temperament that demonstrates the qualities everyone has been seeking. These actions are done instinctively and not as an impulse being motivated for a specific reason.

> ***Love suffereth long, and is kind; love envieth not; love vaunteth not itself, is not puffed up,***
>
> ***Doth not behave itself unseemly, seeketh not her own, is not easily provoked, thinketh no evil;***

> *Rejoiceth not in iniquity, but rejoiceth in the truth;*
>
> *Beareth all things, believeth all things, hopeth all things, and endureth all things.*
>
> *Love never faileth: but whether there be prophecies, they shall fail; whether there be tongues, they shall cease; whether there be knowledge, it shall vanish away.*
>
> *For we know in part, and we prophesy in part,*
>
> *But when that which is perfect is come, then that which is in part shall be done away.*
>
> *When I was a child, I spake as a child, I understood as a child, I thought as a child: but when I became a man, I put away childish things,*
>
> *For now we see through a glass darkly; but then face to face: now I know in part; but then shall I know even as also I am known.*
>
> *And now abideth faith, hope, love, these three; but the greatest of these is love.*

These words of wisdom are descriptive of the characteristics that you seek relating to selection of your mate. They will become most important as the deciding factor in your decision. As stated throughout the course of this information, to make a sensible decision requires your wisdom to be based upon reliable knowledge that will not leave any doubt in your mind. For the gift of love is within your reach. It specifically relates to the personable traits that draw you towards someone.

Each quality is important to identify because it represents the fundamental nature of a person's heart and who they truly are. You must understand how these conditions form the relationship of love. Getting to know these qualities and then recognizing if they exist is a task that takes time. It will require your personal observation and interaction with the person of interest. This is the reason I do not understand how a person can make a decision about love with only an online environment.

In order to recognize love, you must be able to identify its real meaning with the knowledge which surrounds its nature. First of all, love has the ability to be ***longsuffering***. This is one feature about the nature of love which truly tests your affection because it requires that you will have endurance for difficulties as they are put in your path. Having tolerance for a person requires a special ability to be ***patient*** with someone and have slowness in retaliating when someone is in the wrong. Through this persevering power, the bonds of love remain in place with a continual existence.

The "stick to it no matter what" mentality is the mindset that should be a natural practice as the marital bond is strengthened with time. This is the aspect of long suffering that expresses whether a person has the level of tolerance necessary for all types of circumstances whether challenging or not. This attribute cannot be taught but is learned through the thoughtful consideration of others needs, without complaining or placing time restraints upon any concerns.

Then you have ***kindness***, a behavior that displays the capability to be compassionate towards others at all times. This is important to assess because it does not turn off and on like a water faucet. The only time you use it is when you have a need for something. The best description of kindness is one that has a gentle temperament with a calming force upon others. You can identify it by its pleasant nature because this action is a sincere gentleness which comes from the heart.

Making A Decision...

Therefore, it is displayed all the time as a window into the inner character. This attribute is seen through a benevolent attitude toward others. Kindness is a moral goodness that is not sharp tongued or bitter in its delivery. Through kindness you can be an overcomer to evil with goodness. What is important to know about this attribute is that it has an ongoing behavior which is directly influenced by love upon its existence.

A temperament of love is not envious and is slow to anger. The negativity that envy brings is not appealing in a manner which attracts others towards a person, but pushes them away. Having a mean spirited presence indicates there is an unattractive attitude. This disposition is the result of behavior we see so much of in our culture. Love is not conceited or proud with the appearance of being selfish; nor is it arrogant toward any others by displaying an air of self-importance.

Love does not behave rudely or contrary to standards of behavior that is expected by someone who is truly in love without being a controlling force. A physical example of love would be to kiss or hug your beloved and treat them in a manner that is consistent with loving someone. Whether verbal or non-verbal communication, strong affectionate feelings cannot be hidden when a couple connects in love. For example, love is not easily provoked by the jealous efforts of outsiders.

There is a presence of confidence that is not shaken with actions designed to steal the happiness that these emotions bring. Love does not embrace evil thoughts of someone or judge disobedience in another person's life. It rejoices with the truth because there is value in honesty. The excellence that is brought to life because of this affection displays a characteristic that is in harmony with the Lord because God is Love.

> ***God is love; and he that dwelleth in love dwelleth in God and God in him.***
>
> ***I John 4:16 (KJV)***

The success of your relationship will be determined by the value you place upon it. A lifetime of commitment is expected because marriage is honorable in all. The world has legal expectations for marriage that are constantly changing the dynamics of this union. These change - producing forces are unacceptable as they attempt to interfere with the institution of marriage as the Lord commands.

To maintain moral faithfulness in your commitment to marry displays your reliability as an individual after marriage. You demonstrate to your beloved through these standards that you believe marriage is a lifetime obligation that has fulltime accountability. This is not a temporary promise designed to take up another person's time. Your maturity into adulthood has equipped you with an adequate amount of knowledge and personal experience to be successful in your journey.

My hope for you is that no matter what exposure life brings, you will make an appropriate selection decision for the person you plan to spend the rest of your life with…

The following chapters outline a more specific detail of God's plan for selecting your mate.

Chapter 2

IN THE BEGINNING

And the Lord God said it is not good that man should be alone; I will make him an help meet for him.
Genesis 2:18 (KJV)

The following information has been written to offer a simple thought process on how to determine if a decision for marriage is appropriate. Selecting Your Mate originated from a concern to share knowledge with young, unmarried singles that have the desire to spend their life with another in matrimony. There appears to be great confusion about fundamental knowledge that surrounds such a sacred institution.

This makes it necessary to address these concerns with suitable explanations. Let's take a look at the process of selection and examine how deviation from established precepts on mating is creating senseless decisions that produce difficult results. Having knowledge of these ideas prior to a marital commitment is crucial and will help you confirm your decision or discourage a union.

After a bad experience with someone who was not the best choice for you to spend time with, you begin to question how the courtship (or in some cases even a previous marriage) ever came into existence. The most apparent concern should be your tendency to make toxic relationship decisions that do not become questionable until it is too late. Shortly after these episodes, when the next opportunity to date comes along, you go into the suspicious mode, and you are unable to separate situations.

Upon self-examination, you decide there was not the right mix of compatibility. You have yet to learn from previous experiences not to repeat the same mistakes. Challenging interactions with your beloved seem to alter the enchanted outcome hoped for between two people. Although this scenario appears to be common and of great concern, troublesome personalities are not the only interference many relationships face today.

Selection of a mate not only requires sorting through available singles you consider as potential mates but having an understanding of who can be your mate. For example, someone's spouse cannot become your mate. The obvious reason being this person is already married. It does not matter if they are separated from one another. The fact remains that this man or woman is still legally bound in marriage.

A woman was engaged to a man that she dated four and a half years. After many attempts to begin the process for planning the wedding; and troubling conversations about marriage, the engagement finally ended. It was discovered that "Larry", the intended fiancé, was currently married. How did this happen? First of all the appropriate question was never asked…"Are you married?" The answer should include the correct stage of the relationship: married…separated… pending divorce.

Have we lost our way because we take so much for granted? With numerous outlets available for verifying information we are still uninformed about crucial information. There are standards in place to help you successfully rationalize your preference for an intended mate. A criterion for selection is safest when it is based upon a foundation of knowledge that has already been long established. The information that you seek exists within the greatest book of knowledge…the Bible.

These inspired accounts speak the will of God. Scriptures are the result of perfection in wisdom that cannot fail when properly used. Once you accept the value of this knowledge, you will begin to see how powerful an affect truth has upon the conditions for marital success. The first consideration in selection of a mate is searching for someone who will become your complement. As a natural progression begins to flourish in this direction, you will find that your complement makes you complete.

This person is a support and an encouragement to the ideas in which you believe. Everyone should have a desire to maintain happiness that is unconditional within their marriage. Nobody wants to spend the rest of his or her life connected to a miserable person. Besides, what joy does that bring into your life? The Lord did not create marriage to be a "temporary" condition. Therefore, keeping these thoughts in mind, the selection of your marital partner is crucial.

Until this wisdom is respected, you will continue to see people jump from one marriage relationship into another, without planning for the future. You need to ask yourself this question: Is this someone I can truly grow old with and depend upon when I get sick? Take the time to consider the answer. The habitual practice has been a constant pattern of thoughtless reasoning. Let's end the cycle and start from the beginning…

When a couple steps into a matrimonial union, the ultimate focus is to please their mate. This is enhanced by behavior that is shaped through marriage for exclusive joy between a husband and wife. An enormous amount of attention has always been placed upon the conditions for success in marriage but not selection. There are marriage enrichment seminars which include different types of activities for couples that want to enhance the strength of their relationship.

Many of these exercises are the same elements to be considered prior to the final commitment. After all, why would you commit your life to an individual that you cannot connect with under any circumstances? Some people are under the impression that if the sex is good, the rest will work itself out. Unfortunately, this is just not the case. A functioning marriage relationship requires a dedicated effort by the two people involved.

Learning the basic concepts of how to achieve marital success revolves around a true understanding of your accountability to another individual. These principles will frame the attitude for sincere love to coexist with a couple. The following ideas should indicate to you the evidence of readiness by another person for an obligation to this special relationship:

1. Understanding your role in marriage;
2. Being prepared to assume responsibilities as a partner; and
3. Having a natural inclination of love towards your intended mate.

Once a marriage exists, the selection process is completed. Being mindful that every decision has a consequence makes the road to a love commitment easier to consider. The reasoning behind this thought is timely because you are still in a position to accept or decline an opportunity to get married. There is a great assurance in knowing that the decision you make is undoubtedly the best when two persons are ready for commitment.

To help with this cause, you must focus on ensuring that you see the qualities that will be expressed throughout this book in your mate. Release those confusing ideas which have been imprinted upon your thoughts and interfere with your capability to accept a mindset of the perfect wisdom of God. Discharge any wrong ideas that are not consistent with Biblical knowledge. Upon this renewal of the mind, you open the door for your blessing to come forth and have the mate you desire when it is the Lord's will.

> *Who so findeth a wife findeth a good thing, and obtaineth favor of the Lord.*
>
> *Proverbs* **18:22 (KJV)**

This wisdom is a basic consideration in the success of a relationship. It is the responsibility of a man to find his mate. When he makes that step, he claims ownership to responsibility because the decision was made without prompting from someone else. Much too often women take on this task as though it is their right to lifetime happiness. This is not the role of a woman because she is not the one who takes the lead in providing for the family. In essence, this is the beginning of the selection process.

> *But if any provide not for his own, and specially for those of his own house, he hath denied the faith, and is worse than an infidel.*
>
> **I Timothy 5:8 (KJV)**

For any man who is a Christian or one who has religious values, this scripture is of critical importance. An infidel is one who denies the truth of God's written word. Being slack in family responsibility is not reflective of a believer's profile, and is reflective of he who lacks faith in religious principles. Responsibility comes with a decision. Instructions are given in order to be received. An unbeliever cannot glorify God when there is no trust in his principles.

Divine approval is granted upon a proper choice. Accountability for the leadership in a family is established when a man chooses his wife. The ability to discern that which is actual truth for seeking happiness is an important task in making sound decisions. It should not be limited to the wisdom of the world. The truth about love is that it reflects a perfect peace which surpasses all of our understanding because it is of God.

> *Nevertheless, to avoid fornication, let every man have his own wife, and let every woman have her own husband.*
>
> **I Corinthians 7:2 (KJV)**

Singles have lost sight of this Bible passage. In order to avoid the sin of sex, you need a mate. Sexual relations are not a prerequisite for marital consideration or proof of sincerity to love. Immunity to morality will make you overlook a question of importance. How faithful can someone be in marriage when there is no self-control before? Premarital sexual relationships diminish the opportunity for a commitment to marriage.

This is especially true when you are in the dating stage. Sexual prowess does not determine whether a person will make a good mate for you. Engaging in sexual pleasures prior to marriage is an action which only interferes with one's desire to make a decision to complete an obligation. Why? Now, the thrill of the first time is gone and it creates an underlying doubt about the ability of your beloved to remain faithful in a true commitment…the marriage relationship.

Trust becomes a continuous, unspoken concern. There is no advantage to disrupting a person's emotional well-being with insecurity about faithfulness. If the sacrifice is love with conditions, you enable a person to walk away and never look back. Avoid these agendas. We all understand how devastating rejection can be when you love somebody and they do not love you back. In this case there is certainly truth in the old adage, "Why buy the cow when the milk is free?"

Upon marriage, you become as one and sexual intimacy seals that bond. Freely committing fornication, which is sex outside of a marriage relationship, eliminates the need to become as one. This practice interferes with that special joy of a one-on-one relationship. Consequently, the reality one faces is that you cannot become one with many. An out of control ego is dangerous. Choices that are based strictly upon the flesh confuse the boundaries of courtship.

Once you become a slave to sexual freedom, there is greater difficulty in making a sincere commitment. Sex outside of marriage provides temporary contentment until the next occasion comes along. Your attention will continue to be redirected to physical pleasures, and you will feel yourself on a perpetual emotional roller coaster which takes you in many directions. The end result is chaos with an inability to find love. There is no advantage in actions that place your emotional health in the painful positions of life. Break the cycle right now.

If you believe that you are the Mr. or Mrs. Right for each other, make every effort to abstain from a focus on sexual fulfillment until marriage. This sexual fulfillment is the gift of marriage. In addition, when you love someone with pre-existing stipulations, you sacrifice the natural success of the relationship and enable that person to walk away, never to look back. The special qualities that you seek in a mate are those attributes which will sustain a marriage union and are enhanced by your commitment to God.

Within a reasonable time you will be able to discern whether or not there is marriage potential in the individual you seek. When you are assured there is a sincere obligation to perform the role of your spouse in marriage, plans for a wedding ceremony can begin. Lengthy engagements are not recommended, as they become a difficult test of endurance.

> ***Do not deprive each other except by mutual consent and for a time, so that you may devote yourself to prayer. Then come together again so Satan will not tempt you because of your lack of self-control.***

I Corinthians 7:5 (NIV)

When you become husband and wife, your bodies belong to each other. You are not to deny each other the pleasure of sexual relations unless it is with agreement. Secondly, this time is for focus upon prayer. Within this sacred knowledge "time" denotes an occasion that refers to a definite period of opportunity. Never underestimate the influence of Satan when it comes to our human weaknesses. Marriage was created for complete companionship. A married couple should not place unnecessary limits upon each other with these efforts.

Each man is to have his own wife and each wife a husband of her own. Take notice of how these scriptures become an important piece of the complete wisdom that forms God's masterpiece…marriage. The elements which are important to sustain a relationship were divinely created to keep balance in serving one another. When you practice these principles, a cycle for disorder is eliminated because marriage was not designed as a contribution to chaos. Holding on to God's unchanging truth is the force that will complete the emotional attachment with strength and the ability to maintain the objectives of matrimony.

> *Wives, submit yourselves unto you own husbands, as it is fit in the Lord. Husbands, love your wives and be not bitter against them.*
>
> *Colossians 3:18, 19 (KJV)*

Submission is a sacrifice made for the benefit of maintaining a life style that is pleasing to God.

It requires listening skills when receiving advice and an attitude of cooperation to work together.

Selecting Your Mate

When a woman becomes a wife, she gives up being single and all the freedoms that follow that status. A woman that is submissive by nature will voluntarily live her life in a manner that is supportive of her husband.

This ability to surrender "self" will only happen when she trusts in a man's obedience and service to the Lord with confidence. The persuasion to yield does not mean a woman cannot think independently, but it indicates how much faith she has in the words of her spouse. Through this wonderful example of complying with the Lord's will, she honors her husband by managing patience with victory and in so doing glorifies God.

Having the status of husband means men are likewise instructed to love their wives. A husband helps his wife to be submissive when he is not cruel in the manner in which he treats her. Submission indicates there is obedience to God's wisdom. It is not an opportunity for harsh treatment. The fear of the Lord completes a mindset which eliminates confusion within relationships by holding on to the order that marriage provides. Harmony comes with this crucial element…obedience, as it changes the dynamics of failure into an effortless agreement of minds.

Only then can a person respectfully make a transformation. The Bible states indisputable wisdom about relationships and studying these teachings brings you to the reality of marriage. You sacrifice who you are as an individual to become a combined effort. The sanctity of the scriptures is unbreakable writings which designate behavior and reveal an insight to the unique roles of men and women. There is no greater example of a submission to love than God, when He unselfishly sacrificed his son on the cross at Calvary because of a commitment for love.

> ***Have ye not read, that he which made them at the beginning made them male and female, and said, for this cause shall a man leave father and mother and***

> *shall cleave to his wife: and they twain shall be one flesh? Wherefore they are no more twain but one flesh. What therefore God hath joined together, let no man put asunder.*
>
> *Matthew 19: 4-6 (KJV)*

Are you prepared to assume the responsibility of becoming someone's husband or wife? In a marriage ceremony, each individual agrees to accept his or her beloved spouse with the conditions of "richer or poorer", in "sickness or in health", for "better or for worse", "until death do you part". Matrimonial vows may be slightly different in their expression of words, but the conclusion will still be the same. This public declaration is a binding agreement between a man and a woman to be lawfully wed with witness before God.

As the union comes into existence you must be prepared to properly meet all responsibilities associated with this level of commitment. You can no longer coexist as two separate individuals that think and conduct themselves from a position of being "single." At this point you become "one" as you depart from the parental authority. The warning implied by this scripture should not be taken without concern. There are many who try to justify their rights with wrong facts.

The question is not what God hath joined together, but the separating — tearing apart — or breaking up a marriage. The reference to putting asunder has consequences. Any time we are given instructions which are deliberately ignored, there are adverse consequences. If you fail to comply with the expectations of this relationship, expect the worst turn of events in your life. Some of the issues you can face may take years to never be corrected.

When problems spiral out of control, they create an upheaval to your entire lifestyle and emotional stability. Finances and credit ratings can be affected when there is a withdrawal of monetary support. Counseling is necessary in many cases, especially when children are involved. Emotional challenges arise as the result of unresolved anger from the failed relationship. In all cases, it requires extensive legal action be taken to undo what has been done.

Dissolving a marriage relationship is done legally by divorce. There has always been quite a bit of media attention placed upon public figures marrying the wrong person. Annulment is a term used to denote man's process to cancel a marriage. You will not find any reference to this concept in an authorized Bible. God did not give approval to the practice of voiding out a marriage which he created in this manner, as though it never happened. That is a contradiction to the rites of marriage.

The process of being joined together was created for reasons of good. People turn around to file for divorce or annulment because of a "good decision gone badly". Selection of the mate was not appropriate for their career interests. Instead of working through whatever challenges have been created by personal choices, the problem concerns anxiety for quickly ending these temporary unions with the least amount of trouble.

What is unfortunate about these actions is how the concept of marriage was never completely understood. It is a union that was created by God, in which a man and woman make sacred vows to one another. Under these conditions, when a marriage comes into existence it cannot be simply voided as though it never existed. You must understand the immense consequence this decision has upon your life. A couple's history will always remain in place no matter what the end result.

In The Beginning

A divorce does not cancel the history; it only changes it. This subject is not controversial. Otherwise, there would be ex-grandchildren and former grandparents. We have added confusion to ideas on marital relationships with our lack of knowledge. What I find interesting is how society will only hold on to the convenient portions of the Lord's guidance; which are those instructions that are easiest to accept.

As a person disregards information that is not pleasing to the ears, he or she supports a refusal to adhere to the authority that created marriage. Everyone needs to understand that the result of disobedience brings about a continual cycle of disorder that can only be changed with the effort of complete submission to the precepts that have been commanded.

> ***But I tell you that anyone who divorces his wife, except for marital unfaithfulness, causes her to become an adulteress, and anyone who marries the divorced woman commits adultery.***
> ***Matthew 5:32 (KJV)***

Accepting the truth of the scriptures is the resolving force which creates the balance needed to make any decision. Its reality sets us free from the bad choices we make on this side of life. Lack of knowledge is no longer an excuse for anyone reading this information. An awareness of who is available for you to marry will make a significant difference in selecting a mate. If you believe that you can date someone who is married, have sexual relations, break up the marriage and turn around to be joined in holy matrimony with that same person, you are misinformed.

As a result of this union, you have committed the act of adultery. It is important that you do not ignore who is a potential choice for marriage and has the capability to qualify for consideration of being your mate. Another man's wife or another woman's husband is not available to be your mate.

Historically, there were places in which you could be fined and arrested for being caught in an adulterous affair and even stoned to death.

Relationships that do not begin in the right manner have a way of coming back around to slap you in the face with the distaste of consequences. For these reasons, it is important decisions are made in accordance with God's will. Matrimonial laws are constantly evolving to reflect moral conditions and the integrity of our society. There are so many issues associated with selection that you must get properly informed about your rights before your decision. A few moments of pleasure can become a lifetime of pain.

A natural inclination of love is not based exclusively upon the physical or mental qualities that a person possesses. The unconditional attraction of a sincere spirit leads to a selection that becomes the influencing factor that tips the scales. This is because genuine honesty (which is difficult to find) becomes comforting to anyone's expectations. Two people that are simultaneously ready to love will recognize this special quality in each other as they are drawn together.

Without any understanding or reasoning, the desire for a relationship just seems to fall into place. What is beneficial to consider in your thoughts on selection is how much you allow the physical, mental, and spiritual aspects of a person to collectively influence your decision. The amounts of importance you attach to these three characteristics determine how you step toward commitment. When your primary focus is placed upon one of these qualities, the level of appreciation for the other attributes diminishes. But, love gives you the balance for perfection in character.

With this as a balance you will survive any challenges placed before you. This is the element that places anyone in a position of advantage as negative factors are cancelled out with the strength of firmly held beliefs. Physical appearance does not secure happiness and it is proven when the attracting forces change... A young couple was just married and was en route to their honeymoon when a terrible accident severely damaged the car and permanently disfigured the bride.

Can the love you have survive all things? What about a person who has undergone physical changes because of life altering conditions that affect their normal appearance? True love does not change with a relationship that is sincere. An immature person will feel less appeal for their beloved when there is no true foundation. The focus that is placed upon a person's attributes differs with each individual. This is the point at which you learn how much the relationship is based upon grounds that are not stable but volatile — subject to change in a moment.

Although these feelings are not true for everyone, they do exist and should be discussed prior to a serious involvement in a "what if" scenario. The burden of seeing a loved one suffer is quite difficult for some to endure. As unrealistic as this scenario may seem, it causes people to react in unexpected ways. Most people are not mentally prepared to deal with challenges associated with injuries until it impacts their life. Are the qualities you seek in a mate realistic?

In the beginning of the courtship there were not any significant health concerns. Maybe you met at the tender age of 18. As people mature in their relationship there are noticeable changes which occur to the physical body. The most common changes being hair loss for men as they age and weight gain for women after having children. As time progresses, your temperament may change into a concern for maintaining the youthful look you had when you first met.

When personal addictions enslave your thinking, the perfect relationship situation can change and spiral out of control without warning. We do not always acknowledge how much of a challenge this becomes. As you look at

Selecting Your Mate

the differences in viewpoints regarding these matters, you open the mind to a renewed beginning for the choices that are made. Until you come to the understanding that it is impossible for everyone to be correct in their opinions, a selection that is sensible will not be made.

After all, everyone is a unique being. That is what defines who he or she is as a person. Having said these things, you cannot ignore who is eligible to become your prospective mate. For example, "Currently married but getting a divorce" is not an available status for marriage to someone else. Dating someone's spouse has a severe impact upon the success of any courtship! Although there are many variables to be considered with selection, these situations are better when left alone.

Our earthly existence can readily place our eternal lives at stake with senseless decisions. The Bible tells us we shall all stand before God in judgment. By the bad choices we make an eternal opportunity can be altered. There is no hidden message in what is clearly defined as God's position on the subject of marriage. The holy union of a man and woman has always been regarded with great honor. This relationship provides historical lineage to our ancestors and establishes the origins of genealogy.

The future evolution of any family is generated from a marriage. Through this union many characteristics of an individual are transmitted from generation to generation. The physical traits of heredity are seen in the offspring of two people, and they are simply amazing as they reveal their personal heritage. Hereditary similarities are not limited to the immediate family circle. Some of these traits can skip generations, showing up in future or extended branches of the family that you may never see or know.

A successful marriage union is not dependent upon any of these physical attributes. The anecdote to a successful marriage relationship is established with a foundation that stems from faith in the word of God. These are the elements that will supersede anything that man says. There is a lack of reasoning present when you allow your trust in God to be influenced by ideas of the world. Why ignore that which demonstrates perfection to avoid falling short?

> *Neither give heed to fables and endless genealogies, which minister questions, rather than godly edifying which is in faith: so do.*
> *I Timothy 1:4 (KJV)*

Selection of a mate is a topic that provokes many interesting conversations. Most people admit some form of failure in relationships, but nobody ever discusses a successful method to use for selection. Popular beliefs on dating may bring worldly wisdom to your ears but it still creates confusion that interferes with the direction of the relationship. This information can dominate your thoughts with conflicts against Biblical principles on conduct, dress and sexual activity.

To reverse the direction in which this sacred institution is traveling a different pattern of thinking is necessary. The continual rise in the number of failed marriages will lead us to believe that there is the existence of a great amount of disorder in our thinking. The process many use for selection is not working. Marriage has become similar to a lottery system in which you take a chance. Sometimes you win and other times you lose.

In order to determine the best way to make a suitable decision, let's investigate issues that prevent a successful union. Some concerns relating to selection are based upon ideas that have developed from stylish trendsetters. The problem we face with a trend is that it is characterized by a temporary existence — here today and gone tomorrow. These are the conditions of its recognizable pattern. Short-lived opinions promote a disturbing neglect for sound knowledge that has been a stabilizing force in our life. When you accept these concepts by allowing them to enter into your life, confusion disconnects you from trusting in the Lord.

> ***Trust in the Lord with all thine heart; and lean not unto thine own understanding.***
>
> ***In all thy ways acknowledge him, and he shall direct thy paths.***
>
> ***Proverbs 3:5, 6 (KJV)***

To achieve wedded bliss, there should be a combined desire of both partners to accomplish that goal. Quite often you hear the statement, "He or she wants to get married." This indicates one person within the partnership is taking responsibility for a major decision that should involve both people. The manner in which you speak of your beloved displays how you truly feel about this person and communicates to others your respect and willingness to make a commitment.

A couple must recognize how their attitude about a relationship can impact the future direction of the union. One conflict you do not want in marriage is a one-sided decision, where one dominates the ability to make choices together. This interferes with the idea of two minds operating as one. The decision for marriage involves a mutual agreement by which two people form a bond of love to combine their individual lifestyles as a compliment to each other.

Courtship has a better chance of survival when a couple is equipped with an understanding of what each person desires from their interaction together. The valuable moral principles that you believe should be exhibited by a person without prompting. In order to be a compliment in each other's lives, keep in mind that you cannot expect another individual to practice standards that you do not display in your own life. There are certain practices which a couple needs to commit to doing.

The following guidelines will help prepare you to become a better mate. These suggestions are for the purpose of promoting harmony rather than controversy in your decisions…

Communication

The fundamental requirement for maintaining growth in courtship is continual communication. Establishing a relationship requires openly talking to each other as the essential action to build bonds and break down barriers. It is important to begin on the correct path with open honesty and a respectful attitude when speaking to each other. This ability will continue throughout the time you share information together as friends or a couple.

Take into consideration the approach you use when speaking. Using low and calm tones, as opposed to loud and aggressive language, makes a difference when encouraging someone to listen. When it comes to personal communication with your beloved, this method will enhance your effectiveness in interacting with each other. After all, you can catch more attention with sweetness or kindness than with an abrasive manner.

The ideal setting for communication is a public comfort zone (restaurant) where you can speak your mind one on one without the interference of others. A display of confidence in your ability to convey your thoughts eliminates feelings of deception. There are people who are timid, while others are aggressive. Since we all have attributes that make us who we are, you want to get to know the real person without preconceived ideas. Everyone is not a "social butterfly".

Some people are flexible and can adapt to any condition or circumstances. Those are the personalities with experiences that have prepared them for circumstances that are always different because of their exposure to diverse settings. On the other hand, some cannot readily adapt to forced conditions. No matter what personality traits appear dominant, you learn someone's behavior through personal interaction.

When a person perceives there is a problem with communication, the first thought that comes to mind is that there is something to hide. Having this concern in the early stages of your courtship may seem insignificant, but it is not. As time progresses the refusal to talk openly about matters suggests there is a problem. Nothing good can come from withholding information. This leads to the creation of barriers that become challenges later on in marriage.

Whatever the circumstances, you are both in charge of your happiness together. A couple that maintains an open-minded ability to communicate will always do so. This two-way dialogue includes comments, questions and timely responses to those questions in a respectful manner. There is no better way for beginning a commitment than to enjoy talking and listening to those thoughts of the one you love. Making a conscious effort to pay attention is an important part of communication.

These intimate conversations will become the basis for learning about the inner person you need to know. Ask about family and friends. Get to know the likes and dislikes because most people focus on the positive and let differences slip by. You are going to find this information to be important farther along when thoughts of marriage arise. The ultimate connection has been achieved when this special person becomes your lifetime partner.

Some singles fear the loss of individuality within a partnership. If this is the case, tell the person good-bye quickly because that way of thinking spells TROUBLE. He or she is not in the frame of mind to begin thinking about an obligation with anybody. There is nothing worse than trying to change someone's personality to fit what you want. The strength that a combined effort of love brings is much more rewarding than having to deal with feelings of insecurity.

When a person lacks the desire to make a mental transition into a love commitment, it is okay, because that is their choice. Everyone you meet is not marriage material and courtship is a prerequisite to marriage. If a person is not interested in you, there may be several reasons.

"Not now...", "Never...", or "I need more time to learn about you." It is in your best interest to take your time because the knowledge you accumulate about someone is what determines whether or not you become interested.

Make Adjustments

Today's marital unions have many different dynamics. There will be adjustments made to your personal behavior when two people begin to assume this status. Marriages that incorporate additional family assets, such as children, pets or even parent(s), require additional sacrifices are made. The groundwork of a relationship has standards which are established "in the beginning" of the courtship.

A marriage commitment means there will be work involved to make your relationship what you want it to be. The hierarchy of a Christian based marriage is God first and then your spouse is next. Having the right partner does not hinder or interfere with this order because this person would not put you in a position that would compromise your happiness.

An individual who wants to be your mate will do whatever it takes to make you happy. This is a reassuring thought when you know your beloved is sincerely concerned for your welfare.

For this reason you have an opportunity to adjust your thinking and establish a mindset to create a pattern for success in your interaction with one another. Marriage selection becomes an easier task when you mutually accept responsibility for the success in your union. Now that you have the chance to modify your thoughts, a better relationship can be accomplished when considering how much your personal habits impact others. Does your approach generate happiness or is it the standard for confusion in your life and others as well?

Teamwork

There is no room for attitudes that are recognized by the "self" words. Any form of the word such as myself, or I in your thinking or behavior communicates that the nature of your efforts still remains as single-minded thoughts. If you desire to have a mate, you must learn to eliminate practices that will not encourage efforts to work as a team. The foundation for a relationship is formed in the beginning. Minimize issues that contribute to the downfall of a marriage. Have you ever noticed a happily married couple? There are two individuals visible to the eye, but they operate as one. Each person is sensitive to the needs of the other.

Make Good Choices

The most important concern surrounding selection is simple. The error of choice brings forth unnecessary challenges to the success of any relationship. We are not perfect beings by any means so, quite naturally, there will be disagreements. You are bound within a marriage because you have selected this to be your destiny; responsibility is in your hands. There is nothing worse than being involved in a committed relationship where a lack of intimate connection exists.

Personal problems are compounded and not of the best interest for either person. I think anyone will agree that marriage is a commitment that is quite easy to enter into and very difficult to leave. Selection of a mate is a decision that cannot be taken lightly. Let's further explore some habits that create selection challenges. For whatever justification you find comfortable, deciding upon a partner becomes a platform for making marriage a game of selection.

Seeking a mate begins with the decision of an appropriate spouse exclusively for you. After finding a potential person, you need to uphold basic ground rules. Look at the concept of any game you play. When you do not follow the guidelines of a game, it ends with a disagreement, cheating or not finishing the game. Success in a game is determined by how well you adhere to or bend the rules.

You prevent confusion about selection with common knowledge we conveniently choose to overlook. As stated earlier, an important element of selection is the decision. You single out a preference that is favorable and a choice is made.

> ***There is no fear in love; but perfect love casteth out fear; because fear hath torment.***
>
> ***He that feareth is not made perfect in love.***
> ***I John 4:18 (KJV)***

God has not given us a spirit of fear. When you truly have love for someone, there is no fear of the unknown. Uncertainty only enters your mind when the type of love you are experiencing is questionable. An erotic love (eros), which pertains to sexual desires, is not the same as the love which is unconditional (agape) without boundaries. Apprehension arises as sensitivity for you to acknowledge, because it conveys an intuitive warning which relates to the basis of the fear.

These are feelings that should be of concern to you because it clearly suggests that you or your beloved is not ready for a commitment. The reason for this is based upon anxiety from what is known. Most important is the reason for fear is not because of them, but is related to your insecurity. When a person sees God in someone there is no fear because of the perfection of love. There is no worry for anything when content in the Lord who supplies all of your needs.

When circumstances are not easily driven in the direction you want, be still and wait on God. Wisdom is showing you that you need to pay attention to what is being displayed by the person's actions or reactions. There may be divine reasoning for circumstances not to progress in the way you want. This is why it is important to ask for guidance according to the Lord's will. The set of conditions you desire may not be the best for you and your trust in God will see you through.

Going against divine will is dangerous. There is nothing wrong with stepping out of a courtship decision if you are not sure. Love eliminates uncertainty, but passion has a quality that compels us to make decisions based upon indicators that prove to be false. This is a sensation that can be identified from the inconsistent behavior that it promotes. One of the biggest factors that decide the wrong mindset in a courtship is the push for intimacy before a marriage ceremony. Many people have been deeply hurt because of an error in discerning the way to true love.

Chapter 3

GETTING TO KNOW...

Teach me good judgment and knowledge: for I have believed thy commandments.

Psalm 119:66 (KJV)

Before mate consideration can occur, there is a fundamental step—getting to know the other person. Rushed decisions need to be carefully examined when it comes to matters of the heart. An attempt to speed up your purpose for a relationship does not have any bearing upon evidence that "time" is the element which influences "courtship" success or failure. The end result will be whatever it should be because of the choices you make.

Therefore, when you spend quality time together, it is for the purpose of becoming acquainted by cultivating wonderful communication between two people. As a result, this gives you two opportunities. One is to learn the true person. The other is to gain their favor. Getting to know someone for the sake of an interest in marriage is a serious decision that should be first and foremost in the selection process.

Each person that is appealing to you has the potential of becoming your marriage partner. For that reason, acquainting yourself should be more than just a casual process. After all, you need to know the person you love before making a companionship decision. Although some change

Getting To Know...

marriage partners as if a pair of shoes, matrimony was not designed to be as such.

In order to conclude whether a prospective mate will make a compatible selection, allowing sufficient time to gain familiarity is essential. Much too often, involvement in a whirlwind romance leads to divorce court due to a lack of knowledge about the other person. This decision should be based upon your own personal comfort zone. To be informed about the heart of a person requires that both are open to share in the process of communicating, especially about life experiences that mold us into who we become.

This particular system is the best method to promote a natural and comfortable way for you to open the door into getting to know his or her character. Developing a reliable friendship is best established when there is no threat of the relationship failing. People tend to freely reveal more about themselves at this particular time because there is really nothing at stake. The level of personal involvement has not developed into a confirmed emotional attachment.

Once you become familiar with someone by getting to know their likes and dislikes; you can begin to determine if the basis for establishing a solid foundation for romantic intentions is possible. Everyone views courtship differently. Oftentimes courtship is referred to as a "friend" status to release an individual from the personal responsibility of a relationship. When things go wrong, the excuse is "we are just friends". Friend has become a general term used for casual association without a commitment. Make sure you distinguish the difference between friendship and courtship.

A person must be worthy of that significance. Therefore it is important to be conscientious about sharing information that is confidential. With all the unfortunate events that surround us daily from factors unknown about people, we should have privacy concerns. Most people will only reveal selective things about themselves until they are comfortable in getting to know you. Generally you are at a greater advantage when introductions come from a mutual acquaintance.

There is already some familiarity between you and the quality of your friendship selection. Besides, your future spouse could come through these associations. Every date you have is not fail-proof and there can still be unknown factors that prevent the ultimate connection. When trying to play the matchmaker to friends I have found that no matter how well you think you know someone, you cannot always attest to another's character. Everyone has their own way of doing things.

Investigating someone's potential does not mean jumping in with your heart. Initially, you must get acquainted. This is a fundamental step in the decision process. If you find there is no joint effort to explore how an individual thinks, do not force your way into their personal space. Sharing is a mutual expression that goes both ways as long as two people are open to doing so. When the opportunity is not taken, consider this a precautionary measure taken for the sake of evaluating.

The individual could also be married, dating someone, rebounding… or just not interested in you. Among all of the reasons for a connection, rest assured there is a divine presence that watches over you. The manner in which you allow a courtship to begin is an important element in the attitude you will have towards each other later. In other words, the way you permit another person to treat you will become their mode of interaction with you.

A pattern of behavior that becomes comfortable is established in the early stages of a courtship. If you are not content with the way you are treated at any point, you must address those concerns early on before the conduct

Getting To Know...

becomes habitual or gets out of hand. After all, this is an important part of getting to know someone and determining if you are compatible with each other. Looking back upon a relationship that failed will help you to better understand which obstacles led to the breakup. Be honest with yourself. Did you initiate, challenge or eliminate adversity?

Keep in mind that you both played a part in the events you experienced. Just like a play, each individual has his/her role. In fact, everybody has peculiar habits that may or may not be within your level of tolerance. We tend to be attracted to people who behave in a manner similar to ourselves. There are some things you may want to consider such as personal etiquette practices, public displays of romance or jealousy issues.

Another challenging point of interest is that the person you do not appreciate could be someone who resembles yourself. Remember, these aspects that are typically seen as personality may be an expression of the real person not readily seen. We cannot alter that which is imprinted upon someone's spirit. Oftentimes a couple will meet, say they are in love and want to change them. I say, find somebody else. Personality is an individual's right to be themselves within reason.

There is only one extraordinary influence that is known to make a personal transformation in any man or woman under any circumstance and that is with the power of the Lord. The past will fall away as a new person emerges. A blessing such as this is simply amazing to see as the strength of the Lord is revealed. Change that is necessary because of personal addictions is different from changing who you are as a person. Have you ever had the opportunity to listen to testimonies about former lifestyles? Perhaps you have, and know what it means to have divine intervention.

Those old habits that were not good to practice were eliminated through the renewal of the mind. The encouragement that is received by these stories is a reminder that unless change is made from a personal desire which is put into action by self; it will be quite difficult to eliminate the existence of a bad routine. A basic Christian principle is to know that prayer changes things. No matter how hard one tries, there must be reliance upon the Lord for change to occur.

Oftentimes you will hear someone say, "I used to until I got married." A statement like this denotes there has been a shift from thinking as a single person into a thought process of partnership practices. These changes are easier to cultivate when your attitude and mindset have been prepared for the merging of life styles. Communicating to your beloved how you envision your marital relationship should exist, is important before walking down the aisle.

I heard a woman say, "My husband divorced me because I could not cook. I told him that before he married me. He insisted that would change, but that did not happen." Although this was a problem, it was not the only issue that led to ending the marriage. She later stated that out of anger, meals were deliberately made which aggravated the spouse's health condition. The marriage eventually ended and the one spouse believes this was the problem…

The challenge was never understanding responsibility and jointly conforming to whatever is needed to become successful in love. Letting go of the past and its mistakes will allow you the room you need for personal growth and then a new beginning can take place. Expectations for marriage should be a mutual mindset which prepares you for the success of the relationship.

The manner in which a love relationship grows is quite interesting when you think about it. Once the reason for two people to associate is established, a mutual interaction between them can occur. The natural progression that

Getting To Know...

emotions take to maturity will begin its course as the love factor evolves. Take a moment and think back to the point in which an acquaintance of the opposite gender became a special confidant. Unconditional friendship provides the ability to communicate about anything without a concern for what a person might think.

Keeping that camaraderie affiliation alive regardless of the events that life brings will help form a unique bond for two people. The best example of this would be those long-term marriages that are happy unions. They fit together like two pieces of a puzzle. No matter what circumstances may come into view, these people remain committed to their beloved. When the growth of love begins, you sometimes get those butterfly feelings in your stomach.

They may momentarily inhibit the ability to openly speak what is on one's mind. This is when you realize that you are going to another stage of caring. You feel different—kind of like losing control. Hold on to those emotions until you are able to recognize whether there is true devotion or simply a sexual attraction. You will certainly know by this indication; out of sight...out of mind. A mentality such as this occurs more than we are willing to admit.

Most individuals who experienced the disappointments of courtship will carefully safeguard their heart until they feel secure. A person will carefully consider what confidential information to reveal in order to maintain a flow of interest. This is part of the chase-me elements...pursue until caught. After it is comfortably established that a desire for courtship is mutual, a couple can continue to get to learn more about themselves.

The fear of rejection is a big concern especially when there has been an imbalance between two people to make a connection for love. An example of this concern is when you have an interest in someone and they do not

Selecting Your Mate

return the attempt to get to know you better. You ponder these thoughts; "What can I do?", "What have I done?", "Nothing!!" Some people are not appealing to one another no matter what is said or done. Your true complement will adore you under any circumstances, whether good or bad.

A mysterious revelation about human nature is the practice of wanting someone who rejects you; people tend to want what they cannot have. Just like a child in the candy store who keeps asking for candy. When the child gets the candy, he or she realizes that it is not that tasty. So now the child wants something different. This continues until a parent stops him/ her from the confusion. What a demeaning position for a person to be involved in emotionally.

If an individual has no interest or is no longer appealing, accept his or her decision. Get your emotions in order and do not allow a person to play head games with your feelings. There needs to be a balance between how you feel and what you think. Knowing you want someone who is not good for you is not a balanced association. When a person gets the opportunity to come back into your life, they will continue with the same pattern of behavior.

This person will have no problem hurting you with their behavior when there is no respect for your feelings. Be strong against their attempts for your attention; because round two will have an even greater impact upon your self esteem. This is the case when the person shows you the true self, but you refuse to acknowledge their dysfunction. God knows when you are ready. The door will then be opened for that special someone who is worthy to enter into your life. You will both be ready at the same time. Moreover, nothing can stop a relationship that is your destiny except confusion.

Getting To Know...

When you sense there cannot be honesty, do not bother. You are opening the door to uncertainty which you will not want. This is the reason for getting to know another well enough to discern whether or not the person you are pursuing will be similar in temperament, or worth the time to date. There is a distinction between finding a person attractive and being attracted to someone. The difference is a meaningful interest which is the basis of getting to know each other.

Anxiety that is typically associated with a new courtship will eventually disappear once this evaluation is positively determined. Where you proceed to go from here will suggest whether you are interested in further pursuit. Hopefully you have learned about mistaken beliefs. If there is a sincere desire for you, there will not be a need for years and years of courtship. An inability to decide is already a choice. What do you do when circumstances go wrong in courtship? Be still…

Make no decision and come to no conclusions. Being motionless with silence provides thought without being prompted by any influences. Once you pick up the pieces and continue the journey, a person cannot hold you hostage emotionally. You know within yourself this is not fair to you while he or she continues to seek companionship elsewhere. These circumstances are the times that never end properly. Avoid prolonging heartache or hurting someone intentionally.

Mother always said, "Be careful how you treat folks." Your actions have a way of coming back around as a reminder or to make an example. There is no need to disclose your entire life with everyone you meet in hopes of finding your mate. When a person wants to know about your profession, before learning about you; it is reminiscent of what was called the "gold digger" syndrome. These are persons from both genders who seek someone to take care of their needs like a sugar daddy or mama.

Selecting Your Mate

What you do for a living does not qualify you as a prerequisite for a good mate. If you are attending an event in a professional setting, and happen to meet, most likely there will be discussion about your careers as entry into the phase of "getting to know" more about each other. This is different from being in a less formal setting with personal interaction where the first question asked is what do you do for a living. Instead, it should be the second question. The first question should be, "Are you married?"

We block ourselves from getting what we want when we allow ourselves to get in the way. The most likely reason for this is a person does not recognize what a good prospect for a mate looks like. It sounds crazy but it is true. Mr. or Ms. Right comes along and you ignore the opportunity because you do not know what to look for as the qualities that identify the nature of someone of potential.

Years later you wish there had been a different decision.

The criterion for understanding selection was absent. First introductions always remain as a lasting impression. These memories become the unedited reflections of a person without influence from others. Most often when you begin to date a person, one tends to put forth the very best. Behavior appears to be almost flawless in an effort to impress you. The key purpose for these actions is to win your favor as a potential suitor. But, as time passes, the true person will eventually emerge.

Oftentimes people marry their friends because they are the ideal candidate to become your mate. For this reason it is important to become friends first. Many of the couples I have spoken with that have been married over 50 years were friends first. As a matter of fact there were many that knew each other since childhood and were lifelong friends. In situations where two people get involved too quickly, they run the risk of a quick ending when they ignore the knowledge of observation.

Getting To Know...

This is especially important when one individual has a different agenda and time is not spent to become familiar with each other. Take moments of time to discuss any obstacles that can become stumbling blocks to the courtship before and after the emotional attachment begins. Getting to know someone will also help you consider whether a person is sincerely interested or using the false claim of being a friend to get your trust for the wrong reasons.

Sometimes people enter into our lives only to become the fatal attractions to our existence. You must learn to distinguish when the potential for this destructive quality exists. A young lady befriended a man who presented himself as a business man; his profession... prostitution.

Being selective in your personal associations reflect how you see yourself. These friendship preferences impact the manner in which others see you as well.

Open and honest interaction is important when discerning one's personal loyalty to the courtship. For each individual situation, this can only begin when you are truly comfortable with the other person in his or her zone of comfort. This is a pattern that goes both ways. Do not go any further in a relationship when this capability does not exist. Initially, when people get to know you they automatically relate you with associations. When your parents would say, "Birds of a feather flock together", they were not referring to a species but your inner circle of friends.

You can endanger your reputation with the unknown character of your associations. Having curiosity for information not open to discussion creates an individual impulse to continue pursuit of the concern; even when there is a forewarning to leave matters alone. An error of judgment takes only one occasion to alter the entire manner in which you are seen. In addition, a lack of communication is your opportunity to walk away from an association that may not be preferred by your standards for living. What you learn will most likely hurt you.

As you continue to get acquainted and overcome the initial anxieties of a new courtship, the natural focus is to find common interests that can establish compatibility. No matter how you identify the association between two people the possibilities are unlimited. Any type of personal interaction between a man and a woman can change and lead into courtship. An emotional influence has a powerful capability to persuade anyone, time after time.

Love has several dimensions that are more than just an emotional connection that you feel.

The most typical example is the irresistible feelings that make you weak with affection. You think one way while doing otherwise. It happens quite often, and it is rather confusing because it impairs your ability to make decisions. This usually happens as the result of an attraction to someone's physical appearance and changes as time passes.

Have you ever had someone tell you, "I am never getting married?" The next thing you know, they have fallen head over heels in love and are ready to marry as soon as possible. What causes such a drastic change of heart? Hopefully, it is the realization that the person you are dealing with has the special qualities of love; being such a powerful influence, it changed the course of the world. When God gave his only begotten son, His supreme gift was the basis of what love is… a sacrifice.

As for friendship among the opposite gender, in its true form, there will be that special connection that unites you when you sincerely care for his or her well-being. After all, that's what a friend is, someone you have an unconditional association with; it becomes conditional when you allow interaction to become regulated or physically involved without marriage.

Getting To Know...

Good friends are like family, that you can depend upon and survive many challenges with patience and understanding.

We each place different values upon relationships that develop with someone of the opposite gender. Acquaintances are usually considered as casual associations. They are usually less prone to develop into a worthwhile interaction. More often, this contact is better to remain as such because generally there is not adequate interest for closer communication. A casual association should not be confused with the significance of an exclusive dating arrangement.

Going out to dinner, talking on the phone on a regular basis and being sexually active do not constitute a relationship...wrong!! This is not casual, but it is an example of the insensitivity that exists when you allow another person to treat you in the same manner as someone in which they are truly interested in, but without obligation. Do not be fooled into accepting standards without an appropriate discussion about commitment, as these actions resemble a marriage without a license.

A lengthy courtship indicates there is the potential for marriage. Moreover, when there is no agreement or knowledge that the person you are dating is interested in spending time with anyone else, there is sufficient reason to believe that possibility exists. An inability to progress into some sort of discussion for a more permanent companionship, such as marriage, is a caution signal. Watch out! There can be a number of reasons for the disconnection.

Many times when parents experience difficult marriage relationships, the children from these unions tend to be cautious when it comes to a marriage commitment. With such a great deal of marriage and divorce actions taking place, the confusion for commitment has trickled down to impact the lives of the children. This is why it is important for parents to

Selecting Your Mate

know what information to share with children at early stages in their life. The breakup of family is difficult to endure; therefore parents should be amicable towards each other in the presence of their children.

The major reason for an inability to commit is that someone else is in the picture and the person is just having fun with your emotions. In this case, you might be dealing with a great level of immaturity that cannot be managed. Many people settle for a course of behavior when they should not. A growth process has yet to happen for this individual. You cannot speed up or create a means for love to meet your expectations. This personal journey is not for your interference.

After a reasonable time period, the absence of a desire for an obligation suggests there is no need to consider marriage as an option. Those communication issues we discussed earlier should make it easier for you to come to a conclusion. There is no need to play around with someone who has a lack of interest in you when sincerely looking. The time you waste in a dead end situation is better spent with someone who enjoys your company. In actuality, the decision was made without your input or knowledge.

Marriage consideration is a combined effort. Sufficient time spent in the "getting to know" stage will confirm whether the feelings you have for someone should be acted upon or ignored. On the other hand, some people enjoy playing the "mixed-signal" game when they are simply not sure. With an adequate amount of knowledge about a person you can contemplate an obvious question; "Is this truly the person I would want to share my life with?"

In order to distinguish whether a direction for further possibilities can exist, the realities must be considered. A love interest that has an overextended courtship is a reflection of what will happen in marriage. A slow commitment process now will be the same later. This person will take their time when it comes to making crucial decisions. You cannot make an individual complete something they do not want for themselves. Their mode of operation is their desired pace of motivation.

> *Friends do not live in harmony merely, as some say, but in melody.*
>
> *Henry David Thoreau (1817-1862)*

The manner of existence in which a special friendship begins to evolve for a man and woman will be unique in every situation. Every perspective of friendship, regardless of gender should be clearly defined in your mind to distinguish a person's motive for association. Friends are characterized as a constant entity within our life that never changes with time or distance. These special relationships offer unique value to our life that is based upon a reflection of the inner qualities we cherish. Our friends are also similar to us because of the common ideas, beliefs and interests we share.

Mutual concerns such as these form a common bond for interaction between people. A male and female will naturally develop an emotional attachment in some form to the opposite gender, just because they are spending time together on a regular basis. Why? God designed man such that he should not be alone. This does not insure that any two people are compatible with the same level of emotional feelings for a relationship at the same time.

Rest assured, one or the other will at some point develop feelings of affection, only because it is the nature of man. When there is an interest, cultivating time together is important in the growth of an emotional attachment. If there is no joint concern for love, an essential part of the friendship will change. Especially when there is a case of no romantic

Selecting Your Mate

interest shared, as it creates disappointment. The friendship becomes awkward and the other person continues to look for love.

The open standards that have been placed upon courtships make it difficult to move towards marriage. One person may seek a short-term physical companionship with a "no strings attached" involvement. Face the reality that self-indulging individuals will stay in close contact as long as this happens or they get tired. You can recognize this agenda by the expectations for sex with conditional intimacy. An unusual disappearance by a person that claims to be interested in you is then followed by an unexpected reappearance for a strictly sexual encounter.

Perhaps he or she refers to this as a "booty call," which is distinctive "player" behavior. This is not the profile of a person (male or female) that is seeking a matrimonial partner. It is a signal of physical weakness and the need will not be neglected. The focus of this individual is questionable and not in your best interest. Having little concern for an obligation is certainly a matter of choice; but in reality it simply is not the "NOW" time for this person because you are not "THE ONE".

When marriage is a serious consideration, a couple should have spent sufficient time getting to know whether their mindsets are mutually shared by both individuals. Keep in mind that nothing is wrong with an inability to make a commitment. The challenge is to understand when to walk away once you realize there is reluctance for any type of commitment. There are people whose intriguing personalities may be desirable but are not compatible with your designs for a mate.

Someone who you cannot attach your emotional existence to at any point is not for you. The warning comes to you after a great amount of uncertainty develops. Within your spirit there is a sense that one's intentions are not being honestly communicated. Do not diminish how you feel by rationalizing insecurity as the problem. The concern is a matter of trust. Being firmly rooted in your belief that someone is for you is important. Christ perceived when he was in danger and removed himself from harm's way until His time had come. Do not ignore your internal security sensations. Actions truly speak when words are not spoken.

A dishonest person can quickly be identified by one of the following three traits: Lying, stealing or cheating. If any one of these faults becomes an issue within the relationship, the possibility for the others exists. This old-fashioned method of character measurement will show you if a person has trustworthy qualities. There is no better way of disqualifying a potential marriage interest than when you perceive dishonesty exists and its reality is confirmed without any reasonable doubt.

For this reason, it is important to communicate your desires at some point in the beginning, and while you are taking your time get to know each other better you can decide if there is potential. Some people simply have no interest in marriage, and this is their right. You cannot impose your desires upon someone who does not have the same interest. Your personal assessment of another's potential capability is your decision to make. Keep in mind you could be wrong without the proper source of reference to use in your decision making values.

Commitment is less likely an alternative for the individual who conforms to the dated adage, "Why buy the cow when the milk is free?" These actions are not exclusive to any particular gender today and have resulted in overwhelming popularity. Once the parameters for a sexual interaction are accepted, you change the direction of the involvement. The conditions for this association have become physical and suggest your willingness to comply with its terms.

The possibilities for turning this interaction into an obligation are reduced or eliminated because the "thrill" has been removed. Having no discussion about commitment during this courtship makes your attempts, at any point, useless. Get out of this alluring relationship because it is troublesome. One of the reasons there are so many issues with the single life is that enticement has no conscience as you are drawn into a web of attraction for all the wrong reasons.

This is not good for anyone who wants to be worthy of their calling as a Christian. An imbalance in understanding the terms of endearment make courtship difficult. The guidelines for a relationship are set up once a person accepts the behavior of another. Making the choice to go into another direction within the relationship without communication creates challenges. The emotions get out of order because now, there is inconsistency with what has been established.

These are typical problems of many relationships and are not specific to a gender. For example, one person is interested in developing a bond of love that will progress into a matrimonial relationship. Every effort is being focused upon that desire, while this is not the case for both people involved. Abstinence is on the mind of one person, while the other wants to test the waters before any type of commitment can take place. "Getting to know" means there must be agreeable relationship boundaries. Harmony becomes impossible when two people have different agendas.

While one person has no issue with freely engaging in premarital sexual relations, the other believes this is the basis for a marital commitment. This will backfire into a confusing set of circumstances.

There is a basic problem with communicating beliefs to each other. When the relationship began, there were no boundaries established. The moral conduct was not mutually accepted and was the eventual result of silent erosion within the relationship.

Guilt will quickly sear a heart with an unbearable hurt and embarrassment when issues as important as these are not addressed and brought out into the open. An individual must decide what the priorities are for a courtship to exist or continue. Otherwise you run the risk of a courtship coming to an abrupt ending. Why does this happen? In more cases than people will admit, the fear of loss is greater than taking a stance on these matters.

The conscience of one person no longer remains comfortable with this arrangement, and a responsibility factor comes into place for two reasons. First of all, you are being dishonest with yourself and your beloved when you disregard the moral standards you have been taught and believe. Afterall, the initial attraction was your standards for living. Secondly, two consenting adults, both equally share fault in a lack of communication.

When a person gets beyond the point of concern by losing control, of his/her moral character, it becomes easier to compromise personal values. Remember, you cannot become one in a marriage with many partners. An imbalance is created when each person has different needs to continue the relationship. A tug-of-war develops unless you conform to those needs or somehow try to resolve the terms for involvement in other ways.

Assumptions are made when spending too much time together. Regardless of what a person perceives as the other's intentions, each individual must clearly speak what the ultimate hope of their interaction will bring. When you understand each other's purpose for this relationship, you will determine whether the significance of the relationship is meaningful enough to continue.

Selecting Your Mate

Do not allow an undesirable situation to continue its growth. The acceptance of circumstances that conflict with principles you were taught create a noticeable difference in your character. You do not realize this, but others can see the change in your personality. This is especially true when your religious ethics and emotions conflict with the pressure to conform. The difference begins with your involvement in activities that become disruptive to the order in your life.

For instance, an example would be an indicator which discloses apparent changes are obvious to those closest to you. Two extremes exist; one is boldness and the other is sensitivity. In particular, a visible alteration reveals normal reactions changed, as opposed to your typical actions. An old phrase that comes to mind is this, "a hit dog always hollers." In other words a guilty conscience tells on itself by the reaction displayed. Nonverbal communication speaks when words are not used.

For a relationship that progresses into commitment, it's evident that some people are just "meant to be". Regardless of the ups and downs that come, the two maintain a constant loyalty to love each other. When the storms of life come, they get out the umbrella to protect themselves. Unfortunately, this is not the case for everyone. You must learn to discern when those times come about and know how to respond. This also says a lot about the feelings an individual has for you.

> *He that handleth a matter wisely shall find good:*
> *and whoso trusteth in the Lord, happy is he.*
> *Proverbs 16:20 (KJV)*

The analogy of a child in a toy store makes understanding our behavior simple. When children visit a toy store, they are excited and overwhelmed about purchasing a toy. There are so many selections in a variety of colors, shapes and sizes. As the child progresses down the aisles, choices increase

Getting To Know...

and confusion about making a decision takes over. Any parent knows that prior to visiting a toy store you must explain limitations to the child before purchase.

In some situations you leave with nothing because the child has become totally perplexed about selection. Settling for something less is not the happy alternative as the child knows what he/she wants. The guidance of parental wisdom must step in to help the child make an appropriate decision. As you seek divine wisdom from the reliable source in your life, you will learn how to recognize circumstances that lead to the happiness one desires in selecting a mate. Without a willingness to adhere to a set of guidelines, the door to temptation will continually fly open.

Having a number of choices is an overwhelming distraction. Just like being in a candy store, when you see all the different varieties you do not know what you want because it all looks good. This gives way to another problem—procrastination. This will prolong or even eliminate the possibility for securing love. Everyone is entitled to have a special complement in his or her life. This opportunity should not be taken for granted; so why look when you are not ready?

Look at a scenario in which you maintain a close friendship with someone of the opposite gender. You communicate and interact regularly with no special intention. The anxiety of establishing a relationship is eliminated, until our human weakness steps in. When the possibility for commitment emerges, it only becomes acceptable if both agree. There are so many different circumstances from which a courtship can develop, until the manner by which people become captivated is interesting.

This is why you as a participant in the courtship cannot predict how circumstances will evolve. You can only control your heartfelt emotions because there is no reliability in what another person may want. Consider this thought about the forces of attraction, the differences in what each person wants within a relationship can also be the tie that binds them together. As the missing part in your life is secured you will find this is what makes your portrait complete.

Take a look at two people with similar goals and interests. To the onlooker, a couple appears perfect for each other, but they do not get along. A conflict of fundamental values brings a natural inclination for differences within people. Even though you can identify these discrepancies, a successful union is still impossible. In a similar situation, two people with different backgrounds have less common interests and goals between them; but yet their unique differences play out as a complement for both because one person's weakness is strength to the other.

God's divine order is amazing. He can make the difference in one person's attributes become a bond of unconditional love; which supplies the perfect elements for completion of the whole, within a relationship. This is a very special accomplishment for you, when finding your lifelong companion. The missing portion you desire for your life is attributed to the success of your selection. Together you become a unique combination that brings balance to the relationship.

A concern that can delay selection is that of jealousy, a condition that arises within anyone who cares for someone. This is a genderless problem with no time or age barriers. Some enjoy the reactions of another person's lack of confidence. Unfair as it may seem to you; this is an indication from which one that is uncertain about another's feelings tries to discern if there is any vulnerability. The basis of this insecurity may reveal hidden feelings of affection in which case jealousy will arise.

Unfortunately, this is a natural action if a threat is recognized. Jealousy is an internal response to new emotions. Initially, it becomes the evidence that you are developing feelings for someone. The fear of competition naturally brings insecurity. Quite frankly, this behavior is not worth practicing because it will consume you and become your mode of operation. Once this happens, the reaction gets out of hand. Some individuals find this intolerable. Uncontrollable jealousy can become a destructive form of envy. Be careful of what you project as weakness and practice as strength.

No matter how doubts and fears are viewed, they are not advantageous when seeking a life that will lead to matrimony of the highly favored. With this distinguished advantage come many benefits. When your focus is upon service to the Lord, flirtatious actions cannot aggravate jealousy. Your walk will not be misleading by a person's false intentions when you are covered by the direction of your faith in the Lord. Be diligent in your desire to serve because these measures will not communicate confusing actions.

> *"Be ye angry, and sin not: let not the sun go down upon your wrath"*
>
> **Ephesians 4:26**

With respect to this concern, be blameless. Misleading a person into a meaningless interaction can be the cause of unnecessary reactions. Be accountable, which maturity in action is. The reality of inappropriate behavior tends to create a boomerang effect that will return to you as a reminder of your own actions. Challenging the tolerance level of another can reveal some interesting revelations about human nature.

A person that promotes the jealousy is not prepared to handle the adolescent behavior they practice. In other words, when these deliberate attempts to make you insecure are reversed and used in the same manner, the impact is intolerable because it is unexpected. As a matter of fact their response will be startling because the actions were not anticipated. These actions display immaturity and if you must resort to this behavior to make a statement, you need to walk away.

The best defense is to never leave the door open for unfavorable actions to begin. Jealous tendencies are really a lack of self-esteem. When you care for someone, it's best to let your feelings be known. "You know, I am really starting to like you." Secrets are for those who have something to hide. If you enjoy playing games get the latest edition of... You need to know if feelings are not going to be reciprocated. If you are not ready to make a commitment, take responsibility and admit this concern. Do not take the emotions of another for granted; the heart you hurt may be your own when feelings are not commonly shared…

John and Mary took the time to date for several years. After dating for awhile, the courtship became one of great turmoil over a "where do we go from here" issue of sex without intent. The concern to determine the direction in which things were heading should not be sensitive when you are in agreement. After spending more than enough time together, one person was insecure about his or her significant other having equal feelings of love. The problem is quite typical.

Mary was ready to focus upon thoughts of marriage. However, John wanted to leave his options open for continued dating opportunities. Meanwhile, an unknown woman became of interest to John. Since both were single, an attraction was acted upon that led to a new beginning. Waiting too long for a person to commit, only suspends your life. If you anticipate that your significant other needs more time, then have an honest discussion. Are you willing to wait indefinitely?

The perception of a friendship will change, with an intimate interaction. Sexual involvement changes the reason for association and the true direction of a relationship is revealed. Expectancy occurs for a romance to progress into the next level of commitment. The natural desire is for more than a limited connection. What becomes obvious is a need to change the direction of this friendship into a realistic commitment that begins with marriage prior to a physical involvement.

After having a religious approach imprinted upon your mind, the most prevalent impact of violating this would be one of emotional risk. This comes with going against the strength of your being committed to Christian values. Those singles that have become totally immune to sensible decisions just bounce back, repeating the same behavior. The conscience of others progresses into the insecurity that spiritual challenges manifest…falling short of the grace and mercy they have been privileged to receive. The emotional roller coaster ends when you are still and wait upon the Lord.

An assumption should never be made about the course of a courtship without discussion. The purpose of verification revolves around the ability to openly share opinions. Although the lack of communication is a common occurrence, which allows a person to not be accountable; he/she is free to continue their search for love when there is no commitment made. However, the integrity of an individual comes into focus; especially when crucial matters for discussion are avoided.

No justifiable reason warrants immaturity in admitting your intentions. When you take the terms of an interaction between a man and woman for granted you make a big mistake. It is important that the terms of your getting to know each other, be understood by both parties. Oftentimes being sociable is an opportunity for good company and nothing more. The problem comes from having the "friends with benefits" attitude. In essence, your actions agree to the one night stand mentality…

Theresa, a young woman, was friends with David who frequently called. His intentions were to become better acquainted with Theresa. She did not mind, but was not overly attracted to David in any special way. David continued to call and go out with Theresa until one day he met another woman. They began to communicate and found each other interesting. David stopped calling Theresa as a result. It was not until this happened that Theresa realized she really cared for David.

By this time it was too late. David transferred his energies for courtship towards a different person and received the desired results...love in return. For some reason there is confusion about when to move forward and when to pull back from social exchanges that have no results. Singles get so wrapped up in the terms of the pursuit game until they miss out on a great opportunity for a relationship that would have lead to the desired results...a wonderful mate.

When you believe that true love exists, there should be no obstacles allowed in the way. The unauthorized entrance of a third person into your emotional space with a special someone can easily happen. When a disagreement or problem arises, instead of neglecting the issue, make the necessary repairs. Protect valuable relationships with every effort to communicate. When you leave the door ajar, expect the potential for someone else to intrude into your private space.

Upon entrance, the opportunity is there to do or take whatever one wants. Just like the robber who unexpectedly takes irreplaceable valuables; an intruder will disrupt your harmony with their personal agendas. Your love is a sacrifice of self that you want united in a relationship. This is not wasted unless energy is spent in a courtship that is unclear. Even though there are those who string you along for sport emotionally, you do not have to risk participation in these toxic courtships. You are accountable for your own joy.

Every relationship requires personal maintenance to be secure. This comes by interaction that is special between you without the interference of another. There are some serious "haters" out there, who seek to devour those vulnerable for love, before their own agenda has been revealed. This is a common occurrence, so it is crucial to determine when to stay involved or let go. A person that lacks action to support his/her commitment to you has an undefined intent that is questionable.

This assessment can only be made from an understanding that does not include your emotional reaction. In a case where an amazing dating opportunity comes along and you do not accept the chance for a possible love connection, then, oops...you lose and somebody else wins. These are the times when emotional confusion about a relationship temporarily disrupts your ability to think with a logical mind. There will always be regrets later, when looking back upon that time.

But moving onward, your romantic success will come when you progress forward from the backward mistakes you made. Be prepared with a different frame of mind as you control the change in the direction of friendships and their outcome. Remember, there is a difference between understanding love and recognizing lust. Love is a powerful force that permits you to make an unconditional commitment to one another. This is crucial to differentiate in your assessment. In regards to lust, once passion is fulfilled, the desire is over until the next prospect comes along.

> *But if they cannot contain, let them marry:*
> *for it is better to marry than to burn.*
> *I Corinthians 7:9 (KJV)*

Abstinence does not prevent love's natural occurrence. Once the commitment to marry is made, waiting will enhance the relationship. There was a study that showed more singles were maintaining a state of abstinence until marriage, and found it preferable for couples to wait. In order to not challenge those boundaries, do not place yourself in a position

Selecting Your Mate

to fail by being tempted to disrupt this order. If you must, hurry up and not mess up.

> ***Watch and pray, that ye enter not into temptation:***
> ***the spirit indeed is willing, but the flesh is weak.***
> ***Matthew 26:41 (KJV)***

A young couple had dated for enough time to realize they wanted to get married. The young man followed tradition and asked his girlfriends father for her hand in marriage. This was agreeable to the parents of both families. The beauty of this relationship was no pre-marital sex was involved; although the potential became greater for this to happen when the engagement became official. This couple was smart enough to step up their wedding day and both remained virgins until…

A premarital sexual relationship by no means guarantees the success of a marriage. The practical tendency most often overlooked is a willingness to indulge before marriage creates a greater possibility for extramarital behavior to occur afterwards. If a person is not willing to remain in control until marriage, can they still maintain an exclusive relationship afterwards? Waiting for sexual intimacy is a special gift that will seal the bond of promise. This is a serious issue of consideration that will be upsetting for many to accept. What is displayed during the time of courtship will be no different in marriage…

Premarital relations have become the battlefield which scars the conscience of many with sincere Christian values. A painful outcome can only be prevented when there is complete obedience to religious standards. I once spoke with a parent whose daughter married a young man with religious values. This young couple was well taught in religious principles and both decided not to be sexually active before their marriage. This was a conscience choice.

Getting To Know...

At the wedding many of the guests were amazed to learn of the couple's non-conformance to premarital sexual activity. This practice has become the standard. Many viewed abstinence as abnormal or dysfunctional. For those who choose not to practice abstinence, the desire to participate in premarital relations is a matter of choice with consequences. The eagerness for involvement is quite natural, but it is not a requirement for the success of a marriage. These couples enjoy all the happiness of married life knowing they maintained their religious values.

As consenting adults, pleasing the Lord with obedience is the best insurance for an abundant life. It is impossible to force an emotional love relationship between two people. The sensible reality is that an opportunity for love already existed, and these two people were ready for their commitment. Successful marriage unions reap the greatest joy when individuals take time to get familiar with each other without sexual interaction. This is a joyous blessing…to do His will.

> *Wherefore they are no more twain, but one flesh.*
> *What therefore God hath joined together, let not*
> *man put asunder.*
> *Matthew 19:6 (KJV)*

Most people do not understand the importance of this scripture. To put "asunder" has many elements…to break up…separate…tear apart. All of which are destructive to a marriage. Therefore negative consequences will come for those who participate in this wrongful doing. Sometimes even the innocent get hurt. Interference of any sort is against God's will. This is one problem you do not want with God — to be the reason a marriage ends.

Selection decisions are made with the understanding of information that we believe to be true. With incomplete facts on any topic, knowledge is limited and you cannot sensibly rationalize a decision from the unknown. Selecting a mate is less complicated with the understanding of biblical knowledge that has always existed. Maintaining obedience to the precepts regarding the marriage relationship will bring normalcy back into our society and the lives of many.

Reliable guidelines certainly bring about problems for those of immoral persuasion. When we accept sound wisdom we learn a great sense of how to discern matters of life. For couples that plan to become a family unit through a formal union, responsibility is the important factor in the development of security within the relationship. There is a special peace of mind in knowing that a decision is reflective of the successful principles that are a constant force in our lives.

Throughout time, individuals have suffered from limited time spent in reading the Bible. For this reason desperately needed answers that could relieve a confused spirit were lost in wisdom of the world. You will find reassurance in knowing that God's wisdom eliminates these challenges through prayer, which changes things. There is greater understanding of wrongful behavior with reflection upon this knowledge. It clears your mind for concentration upon spiritual decisions and moral development.

You have a better sense of control in your life when leaving matters in the hands of the master of creation. Your journey becomes renewed as you face the expectations of life with a new perseverance. A unique confidence is developed when you can listen and benefit from the learning of others without having to engage in their actual experience. This is a difficult process because man is naturally attracted with curiosity to the unknown.

Always maintain the renewal of the mind with a continual reinforcement of truth. This will restore the emotional stability we desperately need back into relationships. Please remember to take a thorough look at the importance of "getting to know" an individual before courtship begins and a commitment is ever considered. This piece of the selection process is so important for you to make the decision that will most certainly impact your future in numerous ways.

Chapter 4

ONCE YOU UNDERSTAND...

You will find there is an abundance of information on marriage maintenance, yet so many divorces still exist. Concentration on issues regarding correction overlooks the one key to enrichment, which is the initial selection. Attempting to make a choice should not be a prison sentence. Making an informed choice is the primary reason for your right to happiness. Selection decisions are not exclusive to the search of a partner. We make selection decisions in all walks of our life and for everything that we do.

There have been numerous books, articles, websites and talk shows which highlight unique ideas for marriage maintenance. Each information network offers its version of solutions to maintain a good healthy relationship. Readers or listeners of this media receive what is believed to be a form of encouraging instruction that offers a temporary quick fix solution to simple problems. It appears that more and more couples are having complex relationship problems.

This makes them primary candidates for professional counseling services. Once it is decided that some of these methods are not effective because of negligence, lifetime partners oftentimes decide their fate too quickly and the marriage becomes another statistical failure. This is an unfortunate experience. When this happens, the direction of a person's life has major changes ahead. Marital success is diminished, and the popular alternative comes into focus ... divorce.

Due to the increasing number of divorces and remarriage issues, matrimony has become a major societal concern as it greatly impacts the standards for family matters, but moreover the structure of family. More people are looking at prenuptial agreements before matrimony to protect themselves from the devastation of the wrong decision.

If you need such an agreement, prior to marital union there must be a reason of which you are aware. The greatest asset you need to protect is your marriage. Therefore, why are you getting married to someone, when you do not have confidence in their ability to be your mate? You have already established that a lack of trust exists by this action. It appears you are beginning an advanced preparation for the ending of your relationship and this would be verification.

When a couple claims to be in love, and before they marry they must take measures to protect assets, this seems like a clear indication that there does not need to be a wedding. Trust does not exist. Instead of practicing the patience to renew and resolve relationship problems and thoroughly getting to know your beloved; marriages are compromised with no hopeful options because of poor selection decisions.

You will find more people are falling into the category of being married several times. Most often these people have difficulty with a true assessment of what happened the first time, so they try it again with the hope of success. I once knew a man who married and divorced his wife three times. The true revelation about achieving a joyous marriage is in the selection and not the correction of a mate.

Your decision in taking a spouse is a choice that you will appreciate once you understand the key which opens the door to a much deserved happiness.

The quality of one's entire future is dependent upon how decisions are made in all areas of life. Mate selection is based upon a preference, which originates with your personal desires. The manner in which we envision a marital union is greatly influenced by the information we receive about this special relationship.

If the concept of marriage has been communicated with a positive impression, there is a better chance a person will anxiously look forward to sharing his/her other life with another. Although knowledge comes with experience, having an understanding of this responsibility creates a sense of duty to tolerate the truths about marriage. Over the years, perceptions have changed because of the many different influences upon the desire to marry.

Many of these attitudes come from the radio, television, movies, music or casual conversation.

What you learn is how much every point of view on wedded bliss differs with each relationship. One person's pleasure may be another's pain because of personal tolerance levels for happiness. It appears that the longer a couple is married, the more endurance there is to bear challenges. Therefore, a prolonged engagement (one year) gives you the benefit of time to think, before the final commitment of the wedding takes place.

This will also become the last opportunity for additional time to think through a selection decision. Time allows the natural manifestation of information about a person to come forth. A true desire for loving someone will not be changed by a season of circumstances. Information that is not revealed during the course of courtship can become a reason for anxieties surrounding the failure of the marriage relationship later. A rapport must be established to verbally connect.

Once You Understand...

The most overlooked concern with courtship is the "lack of knowledge". If there is a need to know something which pertains directly to you and your relationship with someone, simply ask the question and wait for a response. A non-responsive answer breaks the communication bond. Confidence is built with someone you love when there is no missing link of information between you. A mutual affiliation is based on your ability to connect yourself within an emotional bond.

Lacking openness in the smaller matters becomes an opportunity for abusing honesty in major concerns later. The biggest disappointment after wedlock is not having a "complete picture" of someone's life. This is not for the sake of being judgmental but to bond the relationship. You have the right to accept or withdraw from someone when you have questionable information spoken to you directly from their mouth to your ears. Having sufficient knowledge about your beloved prior to the final stages of engagement will diminish the chance for future heartbreak.

Pre-marital counseling with a qualified professional will help you prepare for a more intimate connection through communication. By no means is anybody perfect, so being equipped for the unexpected with wisdom is good. None of us are in a position to cast the stones of criticism. Each relationship choice produces a learning experience from which the mind develops a unique blueprint for lifelong attitudes. Take for instance a person who enjoys flirting with your feelings.

This is generally not a person who is ready to settle down. Protect your feelings with caution, as this person is unsure of what he or she wants. You also need to consider that this person may not be a compliment to your life. When an interaction with someone does not have the natural ability to flow together, there may be a reason beyond your knowledge and you are being redirected. Do not be offended because that individual has a right to make this choice and forcing the issue pushes them further away.

Selecting Your Mate

When you want appropriate ideas on marriage selection, consider the source of knowledge. The basis of the information someone shares with you should be dependable and encouraging. Marriages truly suffer when one allows the errors of others or their personal dilemmas to have such an imprint upon you, that it becomes the blueprint to your life. In other words, do not take on someone else's challenges as if they were yours.

Nothing good develops from negative input about the way a marriage should exist; especially when it comes from the thoughts of a person who had numerous relationship failures. You must be cautious in taking on someone's emotional baggage that you have not experienced. Instead, replace the wisdom in your mind to extract a positive lesson from each negative experience. Expression of these opinions, belong to that person exclusively in their journey towards a process of maturity.

When soliciting advice from a trusted confidant, remember a person shares from his or her personal circle of experience. As you embrace wisdom, make sure that it comes from a sound resource. Whether a biblical influence or a worldly opinion, the choice you make will determine the success or failure of the relationship. In view of this way of thinking, you will find the only answers that make sense are those based upon the author of marriage.

You do not want to bring the inception of wrong attitudes into your life with your beloved. The excess accumulation of disturbing courtship challenges brings forth a way of behaving that might be keeping you from a love interest, or one from coming forth. Relationships suffer when you allow the errors of others to impact your belief. Equip yourself with information that leads to a positive understanding of marital responsibilities.

Although ideas which promote success in love are preferred, you cannot totally discharge how the negative side impacts the conditions for a rewarding union. A typical example of negative input comes from a person who speaks unfavorably about his or her spouse. Rather than make a complaint to you about their spouse, this person should communicate directly with his or her partner about their personal problems.

In generally, most people speak of valuable learning experiences they want to share. If the personal occurrence is not of benefit to you in your situation and it creates an apprehension that is confusing, why listen? Most people do not realize that sometimes a problem is unique to a particular relationship. It relates to specific circumstances for reasons unknown to you. A complete reenactment of what actually happened is not given because it is impossible to convey. The biased opinion of each one limits the accuracy of their viewpoint.

Do not become the carrier of baggage for someone else's problems. No matter what obstacles you come into contact with, the destiny for your personal level of happiness is controlled by you. If your interaction during courtship becomes a perpetual problem, my suggestion is to walk away because that is a struggle you do not want. Put your energy into a courtship with someone that you consider worthwhile; and does not have a troublesome character.

The testimonies of Christ have been written as a means by which we learn how the Lord reveals His will to be applied in our life. Through this wisdom, you form a foundation which is the basis of many of the ideas you have been taught. Your belief in marriage should originate with strong commitment to God first. This source of essential knowledge has produced loving marriages which bring about a continual source of joy, because of the order it produces in the relationship.

Another important point of consideration is that unity within a "marriage" is established in the beginning, with the "courtship" phase of a relationship.

The ground rules which establish this special harmony will come from your ability to be aware of how to deal with personal matters in a way that is pleasing to God. Conversation and demeanor reflect the mindset of this character.

> *He that handleth a matter wisely shall find good:*
> *and whoso trusteth in the Lord, happy is he.*
> *Proverbs 16:20 (KJV)*

Having this information does not change the fact that many unhappy unions will still come into existence, as couples reject the advice of good judgment. An inability to submit to God's Divine prescription will bring forth challenges when instructions are not used as a form of guidance. Our trust displays our confidence, and the benefit of trust is not based upon the wisdom of the world, but the wisdom of God.

The needs of self and a prospective mate are important to acknowledge when seeking a marriage partner. These two concerns must be a balanced effort to accommodate the desire of each person without conflict. After discussion with couples that have been married for many years, I have come to this conclusion; the happiest couples respect each other in all areas of their relationship, but first and foremost is their relationship with God.

The following passage is for your knowledge from the book of Romans 1:22-32 which reads:

> *Professing themselves to be wise, they became fools,*
>
> *And changed the glory of the uncorruptible God into an image made like to corruptible man, and to birds, and four footed beasts, and creeping things*

Wherefore God also gave them up to uncleanness through the lusts of their own hearts, to dishonour their own bodies between themselves:

Who changed the truth of God into a lie, and worshipped and served the creature more than the Creator, who is blessed forever. Amen.

For this cause God gave them up unto vile affections: for even their women did change the natural use into that which is against nature:

And likewise also the men, leaving the natural use of the woman, burned in their lust one toward another; men with men working that which is unseemly, and receiving in themselves that recompence of their error which was meet.

And even as they did not like to retain God in their knowledge, God gave them over to a reprobate mind, to do those things which are not convenient;

Being filled with all unrighteousness, fornication, wickedness, covetousness, maliciousness; full of envy, murder, debate, deceit, malignity; whisperers,

Backbiters, haters of God, despiteful, proud, boasters, inventors of evil things, disobedient to parents,

Without understanding, covenant breakers, without natural affection, implacable, unmerciful:

> *Who knowing the judgment of God, that they which commit such things are worthy of death, not only do the same, but have pleasure in them that do them.*

Man, is naturally attracted to the opposite gender as God designed. The laws of nature dictate this reality. You will never see an unnatural selection of animals mating, such as an elephant with a giraffe or even a dog with a mouse. This works against the instinctive order of these animals. Same sex unions are an abomination to the Lord, and represent a way of living that will be the termination of your existence.

This lifestyle is reminiscent of the sin that occurred in Sodom and Gommorah; where sexual immorality was put into practice with such blatant disrespect until the land was destroyed by fire. Are we living in a modern day Sodom and Gommorah? Participants in these behaviors have chosen to become slaves to a way of life that the Lord commands us against…to be a servant of sin.

Involvement in this practice puts you in a position of being without protection because of the Lord's condemnation of shameless lust. God will judge righteously because this is not a union that is proper in accordance with his will for marriage.

> *For it had been better for them not to have known the way of righteousness, then, after they have known it, to turn from the holy commandment delivered unto them.*
>
> *II Peter 2:21*

For the sake of sensible reasoning, God's plan for marriage, between a man and woman must be respected. Any other conditions come from a position that is not God-centered. The concept of marriage was created for a man and a woman to be joined together as one and not with all others. There are some cultures which believe a marriage relationship involves the entire family. Instead of symbolically marrying into the family you marry with the responsibility of family members as dependents.

In Old Testament times, parents chose a mate for their son who could best adapt to the family. Selection consideration included the interaction of both mother — in-law and sister(s)-in-laws. Families have plenty of challenges with just their personal differences. Bringing a new addition, especially another woman into the clan presents a sensitive transition; even for families today.

The family tree is not to be confused with the one-on-one union of a man and a woman. I have not been aware of a marriage which ended in divorce to have any responsibility for divorcing the in-laws as well. In the news media, there was once a story about someone getting divorced and divorcing the in-laws. These are the kind of thoughtless ideas which interfere with understanding the hierarchy of relationships in order to be successful.

A couple can never change the personal history that is attached to a marriage decision, especially with their children. The family structure will always remain the same for your natural born offspring. Relatives do not go into the status of becoming an "ex" or "former". The label for children does no change with spouses. There is no "former" father status or even ex-grandmothers. All of this seems ludicrous, but imagine introducing your family members as an ex-sister or former mother? It is impossible because blood is the tie that binds.

There is an old African adage that simply states, *"The family tree may bend, but it never breaks..."* What a true representation of the family unit. You cannot eliminate the lineage of ancestors; you can only change its future direction. God's design for the family heritage cannot be altered by any means of man. This is a powerful realization to comprehend and accept as man keeps trying to alter the will of God.

While socializing through different activities such as singles events, church socials, career workshops, etc., you may stumble upon a love interest. Some describe the initial attraction as a strong magnetic pull towards another or intense feelings without reason. Others get "butterflies in the stomach" whenever they think about or see this person. Falling in love is an experience you will never forget.

Once you recognize these feelings are not going away, you naturally begin to assess the possibilities for more commitment in the relationship. Take the time you need to ensure this is the direction in which you want to travel with a person. Some people step into our life for only a moment and are not meant to stay for very long; while others become part of our heritage. In either case, both become a portion of our life's personal history.

These are powerful thoughts to consider when you take into account how crucial the interaction with others is to the impression that is left upon our recollection of life. This memory holds knowledge that may have only been a moment of time in occurrence, but is the reflection of someone's lifetime experience that can be retrieved whenever necessary. Hopefully, you will not allow negative incidents to interfere with selection decisions.

Emotional feelings are unpredictable as they can disappear as quickly as they appear. Have you had someone hurt you so badly that you could not forget what happened? The once enjoyed friendship no longer exists. You overcome this by coming to terms with the basics of forgiveness. If you do not forgive, you cannot be forgiven. Only your lack of effort will place you in the wrong position to bring about heartache.

> ***Judge not, and ye shall be judged; condemn not, and ye shall not be condemned; forgive and ye shall be forgiven.***
>
> Luke 6:37 (KJV)

Take time with the development of an emotional attachment, and be sure the conditions for the interaction agree with the terms of how you both want to step forward into your future. A courtship involves two people who agree on the terms of the relationship as it should exist. False emotions can easily be detected by the motivation that triggers them. A catalyst is the means by which you cause a reaction, as it stimulates a change in the person.

This transformation alters the way one interacts in a particular situation. These are the times when you can see whether the conditions for love will truly remain regardless of circumstances. To better explain this idea, let's say the catalyst is money. If someone were to say they are a lonely millionaire looking for a spouse, what reaction will he/she get from other singles?

There would be mass hysteria and probably no concern for qualifying that individual. Money becomes the motivation. Now, let's imagine the source of money no longer existed, because of a bad investment or economic conditions which leave the person with no financial resources. Do you think it will have an impact upon the love? If the individual alters their behavior, then you have a problem; otherwise you may have found love.

By assessing these conditions, you know what is best for you, and hopefully you will uphold that knowledge. By going forward in the decision means you have confirmation of a commitment. This is why respectable men ask for their beloved's hand in marriage and both families meet to make the engagement official. This is verbal confirmation with a witness. In a case where parents are deceased it would be a respected family member.

Selecting Your Mate

The basis for interest in a person will determine if that individual stays around or gets out of town when challenges come. Conditions change and the commitment dissolves. In traditional wedding vows it states "for richer or for poorer..." If the desire to uphold this vow is not within the conscience of a person in courtship, then certainly a committed relationship is out of the question.

When you have determined that a sincere desire does not exist, this should be a signal to change direction in your manner of association. Love cannot be put on one moment and taken off the next, like the clothing you wear. Misleading behavior is intentional and revealed upon holding onto wisdom which strengthens you. After spending sufficient time with someone that you have grown to love, a marital consideration is vital for continuation.

There is no reason for you to date someone and fall in love without a commitment. What would be the respectable reason for you to continue in a one on one relationship? The relationship is one-sided because the only person in love is you, and your presence is keeping someone company until ... You must move on to make room for the appropriate opportunity to come along. These ground rules apply to all that trust in the Lord.

As you know one of the widespread addictions for many individuals in selecting a mate is the physical appearance. If the visual attraction changes, what remains? An emotional decision based on physical appearance will eventually manifest itself with confusion. Someone else who is better looking or equally attractive comes along, and you are quickly forgotten. To learn how another views the existence of their mate is a benefit that allows further options to be explored when the potential of a mate is not agreeable.

Look realistically at yourself and be honest. Ask yourself these five questions:

Once You Understand...

1. What moral values are important to you and do you reflect what you believe?
2. What are the most appealing attributes you possess that would entice someone to be interested in a sincere commitment with you?
3. When do you feel you will be ready to share your life with someone?
4. Where do you see yourself in twenty years?
5. Why do you want to share your life with someone?

Take these questions and consider both negative and positive responses. We all have idiosyncrasies and some need adjusting. When reviewing your answers, would you be married to yourself? Look at yourself realistically and be honest. If you have excessive negative answers reconsider your thoughts of searching for a mate. You need to achieve satisfaction with self and like who you are first and foremost. Then you can walk in the direction of your blessing.

Every potential selection decision leaves you with a new experience, which influences the ability to reason. Having excessive courtship encounters adds to the confusing pattern that promotes uncertainty in the ability to make a selection. Since the average person does not know what to take into account, most people look at attributes they consider positive. Those tendencies are not based upon any criteria except your personal preferences.

Confirmation of this is based upon many difficult dating disasters which stand out to you as a reminder not to carry this experience into future associations because it did not work as expected. Hopefully these incidents will not become a scar in your life, but the memory of a time you reflect upon as growth. Ignoring the reality that barriers exist as life learning obstacles is a mistake. When a selection is made, both individuals should mutually agree their preference is with this conviction; the final decision is best.

You need to grow into an awareness of how to determine the character of a person and turn these occurrences around in your mind to become the potential for a new beginning. In order to change the direction of courtship experience, you must stop getting involved with people who take your life away with their incredible drama. Unfortunately, this is a problem which pulls you away from a focus on positive advantages in other areas of life.

Making a decision that is not agreeable to either individual will become a source of conflict. In order to avoid challenges that come with denial, there must be an appropriate and respectful ending to the courtship. Ending a relationship should not be difficult when you are considerate of the other person by being honest and upfront about your feelings.

Exercising this option is the anecdote that will calm the spirit through the act of kindness.

One of the most prevalent reasons for drama in a relationship is when a person has been misleading in their actions that have extended over a period of time. When there is a lack of honest disclosure about the affection you feel for someone, it only creates challenges when you date longer than the value of the relationship. Although this is a difficult task, once you properly come to an ending and a person still harbors anger, the problem is his or her inheritance only. This is not a mindset that is pleasing to God.

Some believe that the fear of rejection is what leads to insecurity about commitment. The actual truth is that when you make your selection, apprehension suggests that you already sense from what you know that a selection will not work. Quite frankly, you need to have a common focus that is of enough importance to bring you together and keep you both interested in each other. No individual should remain in a relationship that is psychologically unhealthy.

As you can see, there are many reasons why communication is of great importance. A refusal to communicate is a matter of choice. The nature of why there is failure to express feelings is a factor which you cannot resolve. If this silence does exist, leave the person alone because there may be unknown challenges you do not need to deal with. There is no need to pursue time with an association that has no future except for the purpose of being sociable.

Gloria and Tom dated throughout high school and college years. Everyone believed this couple would marry after completing college. In the meantime, "Mary" comes along and obtains the interest of Tom. Eventually, Gloria and Tom break up ending a courtship of eight years. Mary and Tom get married. Gloria was filled with such heartache that it lead to a mental breakdown. My father once told me that dating is for the purpose of marriage. I guess he was right…

How do you avoid these types of experiences? Do not leave an open opportunity for dangerous vulnerability in love. There's an old saying that when you think too long you will think wrong. Dating has an intention, and that should include a reasonable time limit in which you get to know someone. Everyone has a desire to be blessed with a loving partner, so do not make unnecessary steps too quickly, that result in foolish decisions.

An example would be portraying that of a spouse without commitment to marriage. Oftentimes a person will become possessive with an association as if an interest is officially established. But, there is a time for everything and we must be patient and wait upon the Lord. Scripture tells us to pray without ceasing. The benefit of prayer comes when you completely trust in the Lord's will because He is all-knowing, all-wise and all-powerful.

Remember you are God's wonderful creation. When someone inappropriate is removed from your life, take comfort in knowing this was not a mistake. There was divine intervention on your behalf. A weakened outlook gives you the opportunity to put truth into practice through prayer. God is always a present force in our time of need. Difficult dating situations arise, but they only create false illusion with your permission. Let nothing diminish your faith in the Lord.

Hold on with all of your might to the principles which you know are right. Remember, that a challenge will continue to repeat itself, until you learn what is needed by way of these particular experiences. There can be no growth in any area until you understand this wisdom and correctly apply it within your life. Once this is achieved you open the door for many blessings; but more than ever, for that special someone to walk through.

Take a personal review of your love interests. Does the relationship resemble a past history you had with someone else because the interaction between you was similar? These situations appear as a "déjà vu" encounter. There is familiarity without any reasoning. Repetitive circumstances indicate that you seek love without understanding why you keep making the same error in your judgment. This mistake applies to many relationships as the same actions bring about duplicate circumstances.

Hopefully you will be able to avoid preferences that do not portray the best results for you. Having a renewed knowledge of selection can prevent a selfish individual's motive from impairing your spirit for love and affection. Everyone that you come across is not a fatal attraction, but many do exist. You need to become conscious of who has the best potential to meet your needs. Regard yourself with the highest level of positive reflection to attract the same.

A commitment to Christian values will serve this purpose as it empowers your determination to be faithful to the order that wisdom imprints upon an ability to make a change. Be encouraged as you maintain a standard of excellence for the Lord. He is the strength that uplifts us in the questionable matters of our life. Let's further consider the origin of challenges in love from a different point of view.

There are two basic components that will give you a more complete understanding of patterns in human behavior. With this information, you can better reflect upon the manner in which you distinguish between the moral attitude of a person's behavior practices. Psychoanalysts have interesting views on peoplenomics. Some disagree about the origin of development, but rather than confuse you with theorists' ideas, consider a simpler explanation of how to view behavior.

The first impression, "**personality**", reflects a recognizable behavior that is visible. We use it to distinguish one person from another. A person's outward conduct is viewed as an expression of their social maturity. Visible actions express a way of non-verbal communication that becomes the initial appeal. These mannerisms include such things as etiquette, style of dress, the way a person walks, or even personal communication habits which suggest a way of life.

When you meet a stranger, these very same observations are used to determine the "make-up" of an individual. You observe a person's emotional response and "predict" their actions. But, by no means should this be an assumption that any of these habits determine the extent of a person's true self. "Personality" does not show all of the dimensions of a person; and therefore it has a limited reliability.

Behavior that you observe is a single source of information about someone and should not become the sole influence for making a decision regarding a person's suitability for you. These actions are simply distinctions that have room for flexibility. All one has to do is alter the way he or she conducts themselves in a particular setting. These acts or process of doing something has nothing to do with the reasons that drive a person to do whatever they have a tendency to do.

But, you believe the person has a particular mindset as a result. The most familiar way to understand people is through the forum of media. Television personalities and movie actors represent a great illustration of this concern. The roles that are portrayed are not an accurate display of each person's true identity because they are a depiction of someone else. Actors are well compensated in this profession because of their capability to be flexible and imitate others.

Take the example of a popular public figure. In this case, you see them in the community and you learn what he/she represents through a verbal exchange of ideas. There is conversation with the public that includes small talk or feedback on community issues. Generally, most of the dialogue is the one-sided point of view of an individual. The interesting point is when a public figure projects a different side of themselves (particularly conduct) it is hard to believe.

Why? There are preset ideas already formed. "Personality" does not tell you who an individual truly is or what behavior they are capable of privately. A common example has always been highlighted with the inconsistent behavior of popular media stars. The visible projection of the role they portray is different from the reality of the private person.

In the assessment of public figures this is also seen. These people typically experience great attention when they do not reflect standards perceived to

Once You Understand...

be in accordance with their status. There are expectations to maintain a particular image in these positions and any other behavior is criticized as a personal dilemma. When personal activities become inappropriate examples, they show how one's outward appearance can be easily misinterpreted.

The second impression is easily confused with "personality" because of similarities that appear recognizable until you get to know someone. **"Character"** is the internal attitude that is not easily recognized. The "character" reveals the real values, integrity and one's intellect as well as habits that are controlled by emotion. Moreover, it is the secret person within that distinguishes the true individual. This distinctive feature of a person's capabilities can only be learned through a two-way communication with him/her exclusively.

Listening to the inner feelings of a person is quite crucial as it speaks to you about their beliefs which you cannot visualize. The "character" of a person is not a predetermination of their personality. I am quite sure you have heard someone warn you with these words, "Watch out for the quiet one." People are quiet by choice and never assuming is best. Once you understand; means you must get to know the private side of a person.

You may find behavioral tendencies about a person that are not detected until it's too late. They can either make a courtship work in harmony or destroy the relationship. Here are some questions which need to be considered:

1. What causes the reaction?
2. Why does the person feel this way?
3. Are they being protective or apprehensive about something?
4. What can be done differently to prevent these feelings?

5. Are these feelings unfounded?

If these opinions have validity, then maybe you need to look in the mirror to be sure you are not the problem. When two people are meant to be together, there is no need to go through challenges. Two minds that meet in a mutual manner are uniquely satisfying without being prompted. Although there will be some disagreement along the way, it is expected as these are the elements which make each individual become a part of their whole relationship.

The best way to distinguish between these two elements is that "personality reflects" a likeness of the environment it is in. The "character reveals" the hidden, making itself known by bringing the truth to light. When you adjust your thinking, you can begin to see a different perspective. The actions that you observe are not always an indication of the real person. Most people never take time to see this.

Being confused by these occurrences supports how outward appearances reflect the current conditions only. As a creature of habit you are not accustomed to behavior that really uncovers the true person. This reality is a point of great advantage for many who conform to different circumstances when the occasion presents a need to do so in your space. Communication is the key to unraveling feelings that many people keep inside for whatever reason.

> ***Trust in the Lord with all thine heart, and lean not upon thine own understanding.***
>
> ***Proverbs 3:5***

Don't be misinformed. Create a comfortable way to convey your personal thoughts. Once you become familiarized with somebody's "character", there is a better understanding of the person. A person reacts in a particular way to circumstances because of the influences in his/her life. Upbringing has a mysterious effect upon everyone's personality. Be aware of another's nature since it is the essence of the real person.

As you mature you realize how much you imitate your parents. You practice some of the same habits which became imprinted upon your behavior because they are familiar. When a person's behavior does not coincide with the identity you recognize, beware of that person. This could be a warning sign of unknown problems that you should not ignore. Misunderstandings are a two-sided problem; someone is not listening, and the other is not revealing.

Your honest interpretations are only learned over a period of spending time with someone "Character" is not altered in the course of a courtship. The imprinting of attitudes began during development in younger years. Since "character" is an accumulation of lifetime experiences up to this point, going back and erasing the imprinting is difficult. An easier solution is to plainly change a person's perception of how they envision a situation. Take yourself out of the equation and look at circumstances from a different view. The results appear to be less confusing…

Matthew and Jean were at a gathering that was attended by friends and relatives. Friends and relatives greeted the couple and also hugged his wife, Jean. Later on, Matthew reprimanded John, a teenager for touching his wife. John greeted Jean with a hug, as he did all of the other ladies with whom he was familiar, out of respect. This was an embarrassing moment for John as a young person. The guests at the event were equally surprised at the reaction. This gesture of kindness turned into a jealous reaction that displayed great immaturity.

It appeared that these emotions came from out of nowhere. Occurrences such as this present an unfavorable view of marriage, especially in the case of a mature couple who should be confident in their relationship with one another.

The hidden "character" of Matt emerged because of a catalyst (distrust) that revealed his extreme jealousy which was not obvious to an outsider.

> *"For as he thinketh in his heart, so is he..."*
> ***Proverbs 23:7 (KJV)***

This questionable conduct was unusual because Matt's did not seem overly protective, but he did display some odd behavior at times. It was those times that should have been an indication there were more problems. The personality that appeared friendly became more eccentric and a posture emerged that made others uncomfortable. Hopefully you can visualize the differences between what is seen as "personality" and what is known as the "character" of a person.

Confusing behaviors can be reviewed in this manner. "Character" is not as easily revealed as is the "personality". You become familiar with that which is visual first—"personality" because it is an obvious performance that displays how a person functions. Once a person's "character" is learned, you become aware of their mentality for right and wrong as your perception becomes the guidance to complete what you discern about the true person.

Becoming familiar with an individual's personality does not determine the person's character. They are distinctively different. "Character" is a reflection of the innermost feelings that are the heart of a man or woman and not easily seen. "Personality" can be easily misunderstood. That old saying, "Watch out for the quiet ones", is an accurate interpretation of how "personality" and "character" appears to be different. The "personality" has not changed, the "character" has only been revealed. .

Our perception of a person is redefined with new information. An inside view of the qualities a person may possess is not to be assumed without confirmation. This is done by verifying the information from a reliable source. Here's an example. Two people sense an attraction to each other and want to get better acquainted. They realize there are similarities that both share which develops an opportunity for more communication. This is exciting as the friendship progresses.

All of a sudden, KABOOM! The first challenge arises; which is a totally unexpected change of events. Statements are made which reveal a different side of this person. You discover that the friendship you have is with a married person, and you are single. The hidden agenda is openly revealed. What a challenging position to be placed in; not being aware this person has a spouse. You must withdraw from these circumstances with this conviction, "NO" this is not right and I will not take on someone's personal drama.

If you become emotionally attached without knowing the person's marital status, the response is still "NO." The strength of your character is under attack for you to be weak and make an inappropriate choice. Exercise self-control knowing these actions determine the rest of your eternal life. Let your rational mind be a motivation to demagnetize you from the circumstances. There are singles who are comfortable with this type relationship because they know what the expectations are...nothing because their partner is married.

For the sake of that which is honorable, make the right decision for the best selection. The choice becomes simple once you understand that if this person violates his/her marriage with infidelity, there is a great potential it will happen again. When someone is willing to have an extramarital affair with you, why not another? Having feelings for someone's spouse is not a natural selection. After all, how can you develop trust with someone that cannot be truthful?

The cycle will continue. How much risk are you willing to take to find the complement to your life? To foolishly sacrifice a moment of pleasure for a

Selecting Your Mate

lifetime of pain is unwise. Before you enter into emotional commitments, know your boundaries and mentally set your limitations. A senseless decision is one in which you compromise your life for less than you deserve. Every event in our life carries a consequence of some kind.

We challenge those moments when we refuse to allow adverse situations to weaken us spiritually. Our emotional life is valuable, and we scar our future with experiences that become part of our character building history. Think about this, you carefully examine any merchandise you plan to purchase. There would be no sale until you are assured that the item of selection is best. Yet, we rationalize people selection as damaged items that can be purchased and repaired to meet our needs. Unfortunately, this is a concern that is not within our human control.

> *I will lift up mine eyes unto the hills, from whence cometh my help.*
> *My help cometh from the Lord, which made heaven and earth.*
>
> *Psalm 121:1, 2 (KJV)*

Remember, your help comes in the form of a spiritual discernment which the Lord gives you to be victorious. Love comes when you assess conditions that you truly perceive are best for you. Before going forward in a decision to marry, you must have verbal confirmation of commitment. A respectable man will ask the "Patriarch" of the family for his beloveds hand in wedlock. This makes a marriage proposal an official engagement for the couple and there is a witness.

The word "couple" denotes a joint or combined pair. You cannot be alone in a commitment and then consider yourself a couple. Something is unbalanced when the emotional growth is not equal because the personal paths are different. Once you understand a decision is based upon how

Once You Understand...

well you identify with the selection process, you will be better equipped to make a choice. As you focus on the selection of a mate, develop a unique method for elimination before a marital consideration.

Once you walk down the aisle and complete this commitment, your personal history changes permanently. A prominent counselor once made this statement regarding matrimony, "Marriage is not 50/50, but a 100% commitment from both." The process for undertaking a mate should be exciting and rewarding. Otherwise, selection becomes complicated with many different concerns that make decisions impossible. Marriage is not the opportunity to train an individual. Hopefully you do not envision your intended spouse as a child who needs to be raised. The opportunity to learn how another views your existence is a benefit that allows you to see how much value is placed upon your courtship before considering a more serious level of interaction.

Chapter 5

THE MATING GAME...

There are scientists who believe love produces hormonal changes which affect body functions and actually cause stress on the heart. Another theory suggests competition is an element in selection. What are some of the factors that really draw people together?

> *Gender...age...level of education...money...religious beliefs...upbringing.*

Do men value physical attractiveness more than women? Is it possible that women value socioeconomic status more than men?

Personality profiles focus on scientific approaches to the ongoing questions about selection. These beliefs are originated from psychoanalytical theory, evolution, genetics and geological assessments in field studies. Data is formulated to reveal unique differences in individuals and their patterns of behavior. The effectiveness of these methods is founded upon conclusions from research that categorizes similar profile patterns. Success or failure in marriage cannot be predetermined by these variables.

Selection of a mate is not a scientific process of measurement. God has given each of us the freedom to make our own conscious choice. This allows an individual the opportunity to accept or reject wisdom that compliments his or her being. Let's look at some of the ideas that are

The Mating Game...

believed to have an influence upon selection. Birth order is a method that is determined by your numerical position within your family.

With this location, a particular personality profile is assumed. Oftentimes, people expect the first born child is spoiled. In actuality, more attention can be given because there is only one child. There are some assumptions that follow the first born, second born and so forth which relate to intellect capabilities because of the order of birth.

The numerical placement within a family may not correspond with the psychological birth order. The apparent result of this measurement reflects inconsistency when events occur that interfere with the stability of this system and alter its efficiency. In terms of decision making for a mate, these ideas may be interesting to think about, but they are not a fail-proof qualification for predetermining what direction someone's life will take.

My understanding of birth order standards shows me this is an unreliable source because it incorporates ideas that have no consideration for the diverse family make-up of today. To name a few, those conditions include illegitimate children, adoption, stepchildren, or even multiple births. This is another reminder to stay away from ideas that exhibits a lack of reliability.

An example of this confusion can be understood from the following conversation. I was in the midst of reading information on this system when a young man, Jim, stopped by to visit my daughter. In an attempt to get to know him, I made small talk about family. Jim informed me that he had fifteen siblings. My first thought was "wow" what a big family. I stated that dinner time must have been interesting in your house with so many people fighting for attention.

Jim mentioned that he and his younger brother have the same mother, while the others have different moms. He also stated that some siblings do not live together, but they all closely interact with one another...

Selecting Your Mate

Birth order ideas are being used to predict a connection for love. The difficulty with this system revolves around many unknown factors that influence the sensibility of this method. There are so many variables that unexpectedly come into our space and sometimes force the order of family into an unreliable disorder. The rapidly changing dynamics of the base of our society, which is family composition, is being altered with lifestyle conditions.

These changes reflect the lack of importance for its structure. As a result of ignoring God's order and desire for our happiness, thoughtless confusion surrounds what should be a stabilizing force. The existence of the traditional family composition is under attack and we must open our eyes. There are no boundaries when "right" fades away and anything else is acceptable. The effect makes our advanced nation look like the one in question.

The oldest and most basic opportunity for people to get acquainted is the practice of dating. As I became interested in the opposite gender, I remember my dad's words to me, "Dating is with the intention of marriage." Getting to know a person and his/her family was a prerequisite to dating. This advance requirement seems like an outdated approach, but in reality is a safety precaution. Especially with today's predators who turn our caution into obsession. It still remains a sensible and crucial practice. Exercising the option to date by traditional expectations is just a reminder to us of how important the values of yesterday led to more successful relationships.

> ***Children obey your parents in all things; for this is well pleasing unto the Lord.***
> ***Colossians 3:20 (KJV)***

Parents tend to share their wisdom as soon as the first crush on a boy or girl begins. You will learn the benefit of early intervention on dating as you mature into respecting the wisdom of your elders. Preparation is a powerful tool that can help prevent foolish choices. Parents no longer can assume their lifestyle is enough to be an example or to create wisdom. Wisdom has taught us to listen to wise counsel because understanding that "instruction" puts order in your life.

Yesterday's protocol for dating etiquette has been proven by the number of increased divorces and other related marital problems. There was at one time a cell phone commercial in which the daughter calls her mother to say she is in Las Vegas with her boyfriend. The mother frantically assumes the couple is getting married and tells her daughter not to make the same mistake she made. Unfortunately, the cell call connection drops, and they are unable to communicate.

As humorous as this commercial appears to some viewers, for others it reflects a concern parents have for their children. There is a lack of respect for wisdom in many areas. This makes it quite difficult to pass on the wisdom that sustained us and our families. Today's courtship practices have changed dramatically. The system of computerized dating has become a lonely person's outlet to search for love. Although some believe these methods are successful.

There is still an overwhelming concern that outweighs the popularity of this process. No way is there a replacement for face-to-face communications. In fact, the ability to express thoughts and feelings to a person that is visible to you is necessary for a genuine love commitment to ever flourish completely. We now have Skype which is amazing as it eliminates the uneasiness of being completely mysterious. Even with precautions in place it is still important to protect your personal and especially identity because there is still risk.

Electronic dating is similar to the concept of yesterday's pen pals. As children, you have a person write you and you write them back. At some point you may meet, but basically you can share whatever you want. If you make up things about yourself, nobody would know. As adults, the fact still remains that you do not really know who you are communicating with until you have actually met. Placing confidence in strangers you cannot verify is risky.

Parents raise their children to beware of "stranger danger" all of their lives. Now you want to be consenting adults and forget what was imprinted upon the mind as dangerous. We then support the same avenues that we teach are forbidden which is a message of confusion. For single parents who are looking for love in this manner, how do you justify your actions to your children? You are their primary example of how to conduct your life, yet the very ideas you teach against are the method you participate in to look for love.

Another growing trend for singles is ***speed dating***. This form of matchmaking has been accredited to Jewish chaperoned gatherings. Basically, each date will run for as specified number of minutes as you get to know someone. Participants have the same objective, which is to meet other singles. There is a great potential to meet a companion of interest. Many different forums are doing their version of speed dating where singles gather in a specific controlled environment where the speed dating system is presented.

The participants may wear identification tags and maintain scorecards. Upon beginning their first round of date interviews they have limited discussion, move to the next potential suitor, and the process is repeated. With speed-dating if you have a mutual interest in someone that you meet, you are provided with phone numbers. The next step is . . . well, you never know what can happen. Many enjoy the concept, while the method presents another social trend to meet singles.

The Mating Game...

How far are you willing to go and to experiment with measures that are not fail- proof? This method is within a controlled environment. Generally, the players are known to each other, so it might be safer as well as entertaining. Singles in a controlled group venue will have a significant appeal when everybody has a known connection. Communication is less apprehensive in a safer environment. I say this in lieu of the ever growing problems with strangers; because the original version of this process included chaperones.

Singles live to socialize in the latest hot spots and meet others without concern for safety. Today's population is quite often blinded with early success and has more to fear because there is more to risk. For this reason parents are forced to remind their children continuously about their lack of security on issues such as interfacing on the internet with strangers. More advanced predators come in advanced forums. Keeping a control on your virtual associations is limited.

You do not need to know a person to learn all about their personal information, know where they live and even watch them walk out of their house. I was listening to a radio talk show as someone called in and told the commentators how to do this. It was done live from the studio as one of the hosts walked out. There are so many advancements within the virtual world until all age groups must step up to the challenge, to keep up with and manage technology.

Another gaming sensation for finding a mate, which has taken its form as a reality soap drama is a remake of the old "Dating Game". By the way, the old version appears elementary as many viewers watch a different adaptation on national television. Bachelors and bachelorettes walk through the process of selection with limited time for courtship. Singles compete and show you dating techniques with realistic effects of drama on television for the purpose of selecting a mate.

Selecting Your Mate

Finding an eligible person to become your companion in life will take more than a few weeks. Besides the fact that the participants seem desperate in their search and this method appears to be discouraging, as young people stake their claims for love. These shows have brought a new dimension to nighttime television viewing for singles seeking a potential matrimonial partner.

The difference between these revised programs and the original version of the show is now the manner contestants portray their personal courtship drama. You visualize the desperation of single men and single woman to find love. What message are we sending about the potential for love and marriage? This selection technique may appear outrageous, but has generated excitement as the challenge of pursuit becomes a thrill. People love attention, especially in front of a camera.

One person makes it difficult to win his/her favor which becomes the attraction. That person gets the opportunity to choose a favored person of interest after engaging in short term romance with several others simultaneously. Each person will do whatever it takes to gain attention until they are eliminated. The process of rejection can be uncomfortable. Yet, in all fairness, may the best man or woman win because competition rules.

What message is being conveyed to singles about the protocols for dating? Hmm . . . just aspects to think about as you consider a selection decision. I have observed many changes evolving around dating protocols, but one factor is interesting. People seem to want **somebody** that **everybody** wants and yet **nobody** wants **anybody** that is overlooked or ignored. Popularity has always been in demand. Be sure you step back and evaluate your reasoning.

When a selection is made from a variety of choices, it presents confusion when the potential for all is great. A person's popularity should be for

The Mating Game...

positive reasons and not negative. Having an allotted time frame to perform such an important task as the decision of a lifetime mate appears unreasonable. This goes against your personal biological clock which will be unique for you. A final decision is being made with beliefs that may be totally wrong.

What you see is an image of something that appears to be, but what you get is an actuality that can be totally different. Unlike shopping at your favorite store for fresh produce, you make a selection based upon the outward appearance. You feel for quality and sometimes sample for sweetness. Here is another dating trend that diminishes the importance of courtship. An appealing personality or having the right "chemistry" in your interaction does not offer enough substance for a lifetime commitment.

Speaking of chemistry, there are artificial pheromones that have been advertised as an attraction to the opposite sex. In the animal kingdom this ignites a reaction, but as for mankind this would be a topic for debate. Using an artificial condition to "lure or entice" a person towards you is a deception that works against our natural ability to love. The result would be another form of confusion in the control of human development. If it's not a natural reaction it is questionable.

When all the glamour and apprehension wears off, reality settles in and the truth emerges that the person you love has some issues that you understand, but realistically can present a problem later. Just in case, you decide to protect yourself with legal coverage. Prenuptial agreements are contracts that are designed for your protection. Why would you marry a person knowing there is potential for failure and there is an absence of trust? If you need a prenuptial agreement do not get married.

The time has come to settle down; confusion should be diminished as selection possibilities are eliminated. A reality you must face is to determine

Selecting Your Mate

whether the individual has qualities that will be your complement, and the balance is your being the perfect part for his/her life as well. This important piece is crucial for you to determine before finalizing your selection. Time spent with your potential spouse will reveal many aspects of a person's nature that are not only expressed by verbal communications, but learned through observation.

There is no defined time frame for having adequate information. It can only be truly assessed by the two people involved. Keep in mind that when you take too long chances are you think wrong. Your final thoughts in the consideration of a mate will be the turning point in your life. Can this be the person you want to share the rest of your life with until death do you part? Imagine the confusion a person must feel when one individual is willing to marry while the other has reservations.

This is not a reassuring mindset to secure a marriage decision, yet it happens on a regular basis. When you know a person, there is an understanding about his or her pattern of thinking. As a result of these perceptions, you develop the capability to sense when there are uncertainties or strengths without a word. Intuition is our personal resource for reasoning, but when accompanied with prayer, this insight becomes a personal verification of knowledge. We have an instinctive nature that some ignore and others acknowledge. I like to think of this as our built-in defense system.

Whether good or bad you recognize the things you need to know. The problem is making a timely decision on the matters that you either accept or refuse and maintaining that position. Sitting on the fence is not an option that works because it becomes the procrastination which leads to a wrong decision.

Your inner strength grants the confidence in wisdom when you exercise prayer on a daily basis. When the desire for a commitment has not developed within your being, do not make promises you cannot fulfill. It is not fair to the other person involved. Once the conversation begins on the direction of a relationship, you need to step up to the plate with honesty or it becomes the opportunity to graciously walk away without damaging your integrity.

Hopefully a person will be mature enough to discontinue a charade that suggests, "I am ready," before misleading someone down the road to matrimony. Postpone the wedding in a timely manner to avoid embarrassment. Both parties are better off going their separate ways. Marriage is a bonding of trust between two people. Once broken, it is often difficult to recapture, yet it can be done through counseling on forgiveness and prayer, more than anything else. This is one commitment that is easy to walk into but difficult to leave without emotional scars. Counseling will then be needed. Therefore, you have the right to be particular about your marriage partner.

Jason and Carol were good buddies before a friendship evolved into an engagement. There did not appear to be the emotional bonding of a couple in love, but more of the pal-like association you typically see in a good buddy type friendship. Somehow a decision was made for more of a commitment to one another. It seemed easy for this couple to assume marriage was the answer. Jason had no concern for planning a wedding and gave his fiancée Carol all the duties.

This also included the selection of the groomsmen and their attire for the wedding. It seemed odd for two people who wanted to get married have only one person complete all the planning. The element of sharing in responsibility for this decision was missing. Those familiar with Jason and Carol were either excited for them as a couple, while others questioned the real motivation for a commitment. For close family and friends, there was no uncertainty regarding anyone's position on this relationship.

Selecting Your Mate

The manner in which this couple interacted was known within their circle of friendship. There was doubt surrounding Jason's commitment and Carol being blinded with a strong desire for marriage. They had conducted themselves as family, with a brother and sister relationship and would sometimes double date together with separate individuals. Now they are in the process of getting married. Before the final stages of planning were completed for the wedding, Jason decided to back out. Carol was like a sibling and he could not love her as his mate.

The most obvious disappointment was for the bride. Although a great amount of planning had been completed, it was a good decision for Jason to back out before he took a step down the aisle and further complicated matters. Although his untimely actions were still hurtful for Carol they ended up as a blessing for both. For Jason, he took responsibility for a wrong decision before it was too late. Jason is not committed in a marriage, and goes from relationship to relationship. In addition, Carol has since met an ideal gentleman which she happily married. Friendships are sometimes just meant to be what they are . . . friendship.

If you have not had the opportunity to watch the movie by Paramount Pictures entitled "Runaway Bride", starring Julia Roberts and Richard Gere, you must take the time and watch this movie. Julia portrays the comical, yet sadly realistic, role of a woman who is unable to complete her walk down the aisle for a marriage ceremony. With numerous engagements, a collection of engagement rings and extensive wedding planning experience, this phase in her life became an exciting, adventurous journey as she played the matrimonial field for sport.

The actual walk down the aisle . . . well, it was predictable that it was not destined to happen. Julia's character would find an opportunity to run away as soon as the ceremony was near its completion. This was so difficult for her circle of influence to understand because the obvious indication did not suggest there were emotional problems that would inhibit marriage. She was a hard working single woman, who was talented, very energetic and ready to marry "Mr. Right."

The character portrayed believed in each potential prospect that came along. What was later revealed in this movie makes it an excellent display of how communicating intention for some is preferred without the pressure of a public performance. You must understanding the differences between what compels the personality to take action, from whatever it is that causes the action to be exposed.

Richard Gere portrayed a reporter interested in writing a feature about the woman of many engagements. As he tried to coerce the runaway bride to disclose her reasoning for not being able to complete a marriage ceremony, he stumbled upon some information that changed the direction of the events. You could sense the internal stress that the character must have felt as she progressed towards the altar under false pretense.

Once you understand the background surrounding her dilemma for any type of commitment, you saw the character differently. The movie revealed emotional scars which prevented an ability to undertake a pledge of commitment in marriage. The end of the movie was quite encouraging because the character finally realized the person who understood her fear. The end result in reality cannot be controlled.

Bill and Valerie were engaged and began planning a very large wedding with no expense spared. The day of the wedding was exciting as everyone was running around getting ready for the big event. Guests had arrived and all attendants were in place waiting for the ceremony to begin. There was one major problem. With all the confusion of getting ready for the procession, someone eventually realized that the groom, Bill, was missing and nowhere to be found. What a catastrophe on your wedding day!

Both sets of parents were so excited about the wedding day that nobody had taken notice of the groom's absence. Anxiety began to heighten as the whereabouts of one of the key players in this union were unknown. Unexpectedly, one of Bill's siblings received a call from him during the confusion. The circumstances that led to his disappearance were no accident after all. It was a deliberately planned event. The ending was truly outrageous.

Bill learned of his fiancée's infidelity with Charles, the best man. Evidently, the two had been messing around on a regular basis. Somehow Bill learned of this relationship. In fact, the day of the wedding he had relocated and found a new place of employment elsewhere without telling anyone. He gave a courtesy call to someone in attendance at the wedding to confirm his absence and reveal his intentions. Valerie was an emotional wreck from the embarrassment.

When Valerie recovered from this incident, she eventually married Charles, the best man. As for the groom; well Bill's disappearance was only disappointing for a short time. From that moment I am sure he became quite content starting all over again with a new beginning. That would be somewhere in another place, where no reminders of this experience could interfere with a new beginning.

An important attribute in mate selection is compassion. It is characterized by a consideration one has for the other. Having a beloved who is sincere about your best interest is a practice that obviously benefits your future. This is admirable in any relationship and shows a person has heartfelt concern that is genuine. After all, nobody wants to marry any individual that puts self first. Just like someone holding the door for you, whether male or female, it is a gesture of polite etiquette that is put into practice and is always well received.

The Mating Game...

The ideal mate has a natural desire to exercise those traditions as a system of habit. A spirit of affection is a priceless quality that is not prompted on demand. It just happens as a routine course of love. Marriage constitutes that two people become as one, forsaking all others. This means your companionships may have to change if not in support of this relationship. You cannot become one with several people at the same time. These words need to constantly be repeated as a reminder of a forgotten element in today's marriages. This wedding could not proceed as planned because of the groom's distrust and the bride's immaturity.

A dishonest element had already infiltrated the relationship before the marriage vows could be completed. This turn of events which led to such a hurtful scenario at the wedding would only further erode their family unit. Eventually, Valerie and Bill would have had these problems and more than likely end their marriage in divorce court. Taking time to understand your role in marriage must be coupled with a commitment to fully submit to your mate. Otherwise you create a marital playground of childish games.

I met a woman named Martha who had been married for over thirty years. She and her husband have ten biological children. Not only was this woman physically beautiful by the measures of our society, but her attractiveness was an effortless result because of her spirituality. Martha was very happy and content with her spouse. I asked Martha to share her secret with me for marital success. She responded, "After all of these years making God first."

There was an internet link that brought a new dimension to dating. This advertisement brings to your attention and confirms how desperate people are to find a mate. The article suggested dating was dirty work; seek professional help! A matchmaker is available and awaiting your call for a finder's fee of a thousand dollars. Some of these matchmakers charge fees from $10,000.00 to $200,000.00 to find that special person. Before you spend $200,000.00 for someone to solicit a mate of your liking at your request, I would review other options.

Selection is not a game. There is someone for you if you so desire. If that person does not readily present themselves to you; maybe you are not ready for this new responsibility to exist. When you desire a spouse, you grasp the value of having a mate and truly identify with the reality of your preference. Having a spouse will come when you make your requests known and wait patiently upon the Lord.

You will see that there are numerous selection methods that continue to be created and evolve even as you read this information. Although some of these alternatives are unique in design, they originate from centuries of pre-existing history or habitual usage. American culture does not ordinarily practice this particular system of selection, but there are many cultures that use this process by force of custom and tradition.

The concept is that of **prearranged marriages.** This is a selection decision that involves a thought process based upon perceptions and conclusions of parents or family elders. Some considerations for choice may include an individual's social status, education, temperament or religious convictions. Most often individuals will not reject authority in this process for selection out of respect for cultural protocols. In many cases they appear to work because there is no question of authority.

Decisions of elders in the family are trusted and respected. The reasoning for this is that the families have your best interest in mind. Anytime there is a forced union that is against one's will, success becomes questionable. **Prearranged marriages** seem to work in cultures where this arrangement is considered a normal part of life where there is no adversity to its existence. In these communities, circumstances which determine the basis for a decision is based upon traditions that are not challenged.

The Mating Game...

In most cultural settings, tradition is an adherence to authority. It holds on to the practice of beliefs, opinions or customs that get handed down through verbal communication. Most often, wisdom is shared from parents to children. Oral delivery of instructions is based upon unwritten knowledge that is respectfully observed as a preservation of standards of life. Continuation of personal family knowledge must be maintained so it does not get lost in our lack of interaction.

As we communicate by virtual means with one another deviant relationship opportunities have increased occasions to catch unsuspecting individuals off guard. This is an example of how innocent young minds get trapped in dangerous settings. The knowledge is missing and they are not prepared to prevent these experiences from happening. The impact of this long established practice is an acceptance that is enforced without your input of personal thoughts or permission.

In prearranged marriages, partners are selected by the parents or a respected authority figure within the immediate family unit. The final decision for a partner is based upon a selection decision that comes from the wisdom of trusted and respected family elders. Participants of these types of unions have been imprinted with these values long before, and accept without question pre-selection as an appropriate method for finding a mate.

Acceptance of prearranged marriage demonstrates how obedience is based upon having a willingness within a culture to practice customary traditions. Besides, it appears to be successful. There is a fear of being censored by the family or, in some cases, even death if one does not comply. Respect for these ideas is a mandatory requirement. A circumstance in which there is exposure to more liberal ideas on mate selection has its consequences because they are a distraction to the reality of these conditions.

The rejection of customary habits is also viewed as a threat because western world ideologies reveal how insensitive this process is. Another interesting factor about prearranged selection is that no allowance is given for extended dating. There is no opportunity for discovering similar qualities or rejection to surface because the relationship is maintained through a very controlled environment.

Commitment becomes the top priority in these relationships and remains in place because of respect. Focus is on whatever customary responsibility relates to the values of the family. Each gender understands their role. Love is not viewed as a prerequisite for marriage; it begins with the onset of the marriage. This method of selection brings into view the importance of courtship. The purpose of seeking someone's affection is to become better acquainted prior to marriage.

Moreover, this process is a measurement of whether compatibility will exist within the marriage. The ultimate goal of courtship is to establish a foundation that will not be threatened by others. Getting to know someone prior to a finalized commitment in any case is of great importance. With prearrangements in marital selection, the freedom of selection is eliminated.

There is no question of choice or outside influences to disturb the process. As our society becomes increasingly global in social and business relationships, there will be more cultural mixtures in marriage unions. Due to these types of interactions, influences upon marriage will be directly affected with diverse beliefs on how to encourage marital success. Families will develop into a unique mixture of traditions that capture the best and sometimes worst side of generational practices.

Wilfred took Marge to visit his family in his homeland. Upon their arrival, Wilfred instructed his wife to carry a water jug on her head as women

The Mating Game...

native to the culture customarily did. Marge publicly refused, bringing shame to her husband in front of his family. He proceeded to beat Marge because of her disobedience. Her screams were ignored as any help would be viewed as interference in family affairs.

There are numerous occasions when couples visit the homeland of current or prospective spouses. It will bring to view a different outlook on their ethnic traditions and your expectations. Sometimes a person will conform to a cultural environment out of respect for the elders of the family. No matter what you decide, it is better to have a truly complete picture of your beloved.

The global combination of cultures will force people to make changes in their relations with one another. If there is to be a marriage with someone from another culture you must research customary expectations. Otherwise you will experience a great disruption in what you believe to exist and the continuity of what is real. Before a marriage relationship can exist, you must know what is expected of a man's role or woman. A marriage cannot be expected to grow with these unanswered type controversies being present.

Another selection consideration that is understated in the matrimonial arena is marriage for the purpose of establishing citizenship. This tends to be more of a challenge to relationships when an individual sincerely falls in love and later learns that the possibility could or does exist. In cases where these types of courtships occur there are numerous repercussions. Unforeseen citizenship problems raise issues with several concerns.

There are times when these marital matters are known about in advance and become similar to business propositions. Some singles will engage in this activity for monetary gain, but this is a game you do not want to play. The lines are crossed into practices that come with legal consequences and

Selecting Your Mate

you will find yourself at a complete loss. There are many victims who fall prey to these schemes believing that they have found love.

This is a common practice that is based out of desperation. Many people innocently enter into cross-cultural types of marriage unions without having all of the details. An individual who does not have paperwork in order, and up to date, with the Immigration Naturalization Services, is considered an illegal alien. In order to change this status to a legal alien, a sponsor is required. The spouse being a legal or naturalized citizen becomes the sponsor for their spouse.

Upon this decision, you also become legally accountable for their financial support and welfare whether you continue to be together or not. In essence, this love interest that has now become your spouse is a dependent, no matter what condition the marriage is in. These are the rules of the game. Like it or not you are bound by them. Most often, this happens when there is no knowledge of how this status causes problems until there is a crisis.

Decisions are rushed because the couple is "in love", and their beloved might get deported unless you do something. Unfortunately, in some instances, once citizenship is acquired, the marriage may end quickly. The responsibility however does not. There is a time frame that INS has for a couple to know each other prior to marriage. Even those cases can be investigated to determine whether there is fraudulent activity.

Frank and Anna became engaged and took a weekend trip to Canada. Anna was a US citizen and her fiancé Frank was from another country. On the return trip home a routine check by an immigration officer changed the wonderful experience into a whirlwind of events. Customs inquired about each individual's nationality and location of birth. Ann stated that she was an American citizen born in the United States.

She was asked to provide proof of her status and it was acceptable to the officer. The officer asked her fiancé, Frank, if he was an American citizen. Frank responded "yes" with his obvious accent. The officer asked to see identification for proof of citizenship and the information was outdated. They were both pulled over and asked to go inside for further questioning. Ann was released, but Frank was detained because his green card was not valid.

Frank was not allowed to return to the US until he got the appropriate paperwork for re-entry. While Frank was being questioned, Ann asked, "Is there something I should know? I plan to marry this man." The officers looked at each other and broke into laughter as they walked away. Ann was heartbroken as she did not have a clue as to what was happening. Eventually, all the paperwork was put in order, and Frank returned home. Ann never understood what happened, but it did not matter because Frank and Ann were going to be married and have a family.

All "known" concerns were addressed, and this couple married shortly thereafter. They both had solid careers and were able to afford the major purchases newlywed couples desired right away. In addition, Frank was anxious to start a family. The timing was right and Ann became pregnant with their first child. All of these events happened within their first year of being married. However, some unexpected changes began to take their course after the marriage.

Frank received paperwork from INS to attend a hearing. In support of Frank, Ann accompanied her husband to the hearing as it was unknown what the summons was about. At this point in their marriage there were no secrets until it was revealed that Frank had some questionable information on his application for citizenship. The documentation he filed from his country stated he was already married. This was not the kind of revelation an expectant mother needed.

What a discovery after establishing a family to find that one spouse is supposedly married. Frank had to get legal counsel to represent him quickly. Although their joint income was sufficient to cover legal expenses for the attorney, Ann had no rights to the information she was paying for. The frustration weighed on Frank causing him to act differently, not communicating with his wife. These secrets became a cloud over the success of their relationship.

This is a situation that could have been prevented. Ann should have been more responsible in verifying questionable information before making such a costly commitment to Frank. The first warning that presented itself to Ann was the trip to Canada with the INS officers' comments and laughter which she ignored. I am sure there were other indicators, but the damage had already been done and the question in her mind was, "what happens now?"

There are many multi-cultural couples who enjoy years of successful marriage. Any couple will admit there are stumbling blocks. Commitment, communication and concern within the family are the elements for survival. There is no reason to misrepresent the truth except when someone wants to disguise unknown information. Dishonesty is a disturbing warning signal when you believe in the integrity of a person. Stop and think so you can evaluate what is real.

Before making a costly obligation, all one should do is hold on to God's unchanging hands. Through this faith you will know the truth and it will set you free by revealing to you the things you ask of Him. Anna eventually survived the ordeal with great strength and determination. The ending to these events did not matter to her anymore. An important lesson was gained by all of the experience that was priceless to her journey in life.

The cultural environment that surrounds one's upbringing is what distinguishes his or her attitude. These influences are best recognized through behavior. Social customs throughout the world have a unique impact upon how we envision differences in life. What may seem normal to a particular group of people is bizarre to others. Habits such as the following directly affect how a person perceives another's actions.

Most people have worked in a retail environment at some point in their lives. A retail sales clerk will typically count change into your customer's hands or count the change first and place it in the customer's hand. On this particular day a clerk counted out change and handed it to the customer with his/her left hand. The customer yelled at the clerk for doing this and said "in my country when you hand over something with your left hand you are cursing at the person."

The United States is best known as the melting pot of the world and is reflected in the multi-cultural marriages that exist. If you are sincerely contemplating marriage to a person from a different culture, you must take the time to understand customary differences. Investigate what is considered the appropriate social standard so that you are not offensive socially. This is a crucial task because some conditions can go beyond your acceptance. When you review old versus new beliefs on partnership selection, there is a great generational conflict.

The ideas of yesterday were dictated to us by our parents from wisdom that was made known to them. As a result, standards for dating became the forerunner of knowledge on how to maintain a relationship that led to marriage. When a young man had a sincere interest in dating a young woman, he would respectfully ask permission of her parents. The ground rules were set forth with the expectation of an eventual commitment. The first kiss was an indication of an emotional attachment developing. There was a step by step progression to courtship.

Today, the complete dating process can happen overnight with the conditions for marriage and no commitment. At the same time we question the reason for not finding our soul mate. We have the dysfunctional order of girls gone wild (prostitutes); brothers on the down low / lesbian women (gay and lesbian); cougars (older women seeking boys or younger men) and an array of vices that make a statement about your sexual preference.

Polygamist lifestyles that take advantage of the fact that there is a larger female population in comparison to male; and internet sites for married and seeking outside romance and the list goes on. All of these opportunities make the culture a questionable state of affairs. Where will you pitch your tent? Will you become an anchor to chaos or make a commitment to that which is divinely right?

Another point of consideration which is more openly prevalent is marriages that represent a global infusion of love. There are no boundaries for finding a mate. With college campuses establishing satellite offices and online studies around the world, there is a lot of intermingling and cross cultural marriages unlike ever before. The opportunities for finding your mate are unlimited.

> *"For there is no respect of persons with God" Romans 2:11 (KJV)*

The beauty of this scripture is seen the diversity we see in the family unit with interracial couples that have no fear to love a man or woman regardless of race creed or color. The results of these relationships have brought a new dimension to the civil rights movement which specifically outlawed racial discrimination. Through the racial diversity of the family the first black President was elected and those that have gone before us leaped in their graves with joy.

The Mating Game...

Clearly God has given us instructions for the selection of your mate that supports the continuation of the traditional family. Living in a condition that is pleasing unto God will not destroy the foundation of our life cycle; but the acceptance of any other standards will contribute to our destruction. The family unit, as God so designed, typically consists of husband, wife and their children and no other unnatural or proposed lifestyles.

Our values are under attack. In the news media there were reports of a man having a baby. "He" was shown in his pregnant state and delivered a healthy baby. It was disclosed afterwards that "he" was a "she" living as a male. What a message of confusion this sends to our children. Confusion on selection must be eliminated. Alternative lifestyles such as same sex unions are unacceptable and have been legalized with a growing confusion for challenging that which is right. The message we send to our youth as a nation is that any personal living conditions are permissible. As long as we continue to walk in a direction that offers no moral encouragement, families will suffer.

The continuous search for the perfect mate motivates people to use different methods. Many singles are under the impression that finding that special person will fulfill the missing link in their lives. You are not defined by a man or a woman. Be confident in your relationship with God first and foremost for this is your key to happiness. Until you can truly understand who you are and what you need, how can you possibly know what you seek in a partner with whom you want a marriage relationship?

While writing this book, I placed a call to order free information on publishing manuscripts. A young male operator answered my call and learned of the topic in which I was writing. He told me about his engagement and described the terms of it, which led to an interesting conversation. I was amazed at the dialogue we had on what makes a successful relationship. The conversation went like this:

"I am marrying a wonderful person!"

"That's great! What makes your fiancé so wonderful?"

"My fiancé does everything I say."

"What happens after you marry and your wife does not comply with everything that you ask?"

There was a moment of silence and the conversation came to an end. The idea that a marital commitment had another point of view was difficult for this young man to comprehend. He displayed a bit of selfishness in the value of the relationship. As long as his fiancé went along with what he expected, the relationship was good and nothing else mattered.

> ***Giving thanks always for all things unto God and the Father in the name of our Lord Jesus Christ:***
>
> ***Submitting yourselves one to another in the fear of God***
>
> ***Wives, submit yourselves unto your own husbands, as unto the Lord.***
>
> ***For the husband is the head of the wife, even as Christ is the head of the church; and he is the savior of the body.***
>
> ***Therefore as the church is subject unto Christ, so let the wives be to their own husbands in everything. Husbands love your wives, even ass Christ also loved the church, and gave himself for it;***

> *That he might sanctify and cleanse it with the washing of water by the word,*
>
> *That he might present it to himself a glorious church, not having spot, or wrinkle, or any such thing; but that is should e holy and without blemish. So ought men to love their wives as their own bodies. He that loveth his wife loveth himself. For no man ever yet hated his own flesh; but nourisheth and cherisheth it, even as the Lord the church: For we are members of his body, of his flesh, and of his bones.*
>
> *For this cause shall a man leave his father and mother, and shall be joined unto his wife, and they two shall be one flesh.*
>
> *This is a great mystery: but I speak concerning Christ and the church.*
>
> *Nevertheless let every one of you in particular so love his wife even as himself; and the wife see that she reverence her husband."*
>
> *Ephesians 5:20-33 (KJV)*

There is a two-sided responsibility that requires the participation of husband and wife. The perception this young man has about marriage needs some adjusting to incorporate his future spouse. When you can truly love someone as you love yourself, you are participating in the 100% of giving to a marriage relationship. This is the love that is referenced in the Bible as Christ also loved His Church. Each partner has an accountability to be loyal to one another and cherish the bonds of matrimony.

Selecting Your Mate

I am reminded of a conversation that I had with an unknown mature gentleman of many years in age. He mentioned that he had been married for fifty years. Everyone marveled over his statement as many people cannot get past seven years. I asked him to tell us what his anecdote was for marital success. He stated, "I have been married fifty years, retired thirty years and take my wife to lunch every day. It's our daily date." What a wonderful example to enjoy each other's company after fifty years of marriage.

This scripture reinforces the value of profound wisdom — devotion in marriage. Devotion in marriage does not mean enslavement by either party. A marriage that centers itself on God is the best preparation one can have to come together as a remarkable blessing. The Bible is the only resource guide for any set of circumstances and sets forth clearly defined instruction. Completely adhering to this counsel will diminish the risk of failure.

To maintain the value of the family is all related to overriding the lack of knowledge with sound wisdom. All dysfunctional challenges must cease that contribute to the cancellation of our future. The more we listen to God, the greater the wisdom that leads to understanding. These thoughts will prepare you for the most important dimension in the selection process... making a decision.

> ***There is no wisdom nor understanding nor counsel against the Lord***
>
> ***Proverbs 21:30 (KJV)***

How do I love thee? Let me count the ways.

I love thee to the depth and breadth and height

My soul can reach, when feeling out of sight

For the ends of being and ideal grace.

                Elizabeth Barrett Browning (1806-1861)

Acknowledgements...

The Holy Bible (King James Version)

www.ingramcontent.com/pod-product-compliance
Lightning Source LLC
Chambersburg PA
CBHW020829020526
44118CB00032B/405